Quick Gourmet Dinners

QUICK GOURMET DINNERS

Margo Rieman

DRAWINGS BY LORETTA TREZZO

HARPER & ROW, PUBLISHERS
New York, Evanston, San Francisco, London

1817

Portions of this book appeared in slightly different form in *Cosmopolitan*.

FIRST EDITION

STANDARD BOOK NUMBER: 06-013551-4

LIBRARY OF CONGRESS CATALOG CARD NUMBER: 77-181640

Designed by Lydia Link

This book is for
Charles and Esther Campbell
(*and it's about time!*)

Contents

A Personal Approach to Cooking

This book is directed toward the cook, young or old, married or single, who is concerned with simple ways to serve food that makes dining a pleasure; who wants menus that satisfy, with the honest flavors of honest foods, put together in combinations that not only satisfy the stomach's hunger but also please the palate and the eye. Such meals are a pleasure to cook, to serve, and to eat. They are rewarding in many basic ways, both to the cook and to the people he feeds. And they need not cost extravagant amounts of money, a consideration of growing importance to almost everyone, as prices soar and salaries, if you continue to look one in the eye, don't.

Also, my kind of cooking does not require hours of precious time (which I seldom have), a Cordon Bleu background (which I lack), or an enormous collection of kitchen equipment. I do own many cook-and-serve casseroles and dishes, acquired over the years because they are pretty and they simplify dishwashing by eliminating pots.

Basically, I cook with a couple of saucepans, a couple of frying pans, and a big pot of one kind or another, plus an oven-to-table dish and a hibachi. Recently, I was given a filter coffeepot by friends who prefer that brew, but for years I made coffee in a saucepan (page 98). People raved about it.

In cooking last night's dinner (for four), I used a frying pan, a large casserole, a bowl, a little pot, and a blender. The frying pan was used to make fresh garlic croutons for San Francisco Caesar Salad (page 25), the big enamel-over-iron casserole cooked Chicken Fricassee with Herb Dumplings (page 51) prepared in the bowl from a packaged mix. The little pot and the blender had been used earlier in the day to make Harvey's Little Chocolate Pots (page 86). That's not much pot and pan washing to prepare a delicious and satisfying dinner on a blustery, rainy late-fall evening.

There was not much time expended, either. Dessert took about three minutes, early in the day. Starting the fricassee took about ten, preparing the vegetables and croutons another five. An hour and a half later, the dumplings were mixed in one minute, and they cooked while the salad was dressed at the table, served, and eaten. With dessert mellowing in the refrigerator, there was time to linger over second helpings of the gentle, savory fricassee, and an evening beckoning ahead to sit around the first fire of the year in the fireplace, with dessert, coffee, conversation, and music blending into the soft swish of rain in the trees outside.

I have worked since 1935, and my years have been filled with dinners that were cooked in hectic situations but were pleasant to sit down to, relaxed and relaxing, rewarding in all ways. Such dining is truly possible for busy people. It takes planning, to be sure, but it does not take endless amounts of time that you don't have to spare or large amounts of money that you don't have to spend.

So that is what this book is all about. I can pass on to you my recipes, and the acquired knowledge that makes them practical. I can hope they will make your cooking as rewarding to you as mine has been to me. To all of you who have written to me in the past years, asking for a book like this, I want once more to express my thanks. Without your interest in good food we would all be reduced to existing on prefabricated cardboard dinners, since no real food would be available.

Although frozen vegetables are a godsend when you can't get fresh ones (tiny whole string beans, little baby peas and limas, Italian green beans, and Chinese pea pods are not always easy to come by, nor is fresh asparagus), I do not like "dinners-in-a-box." I do try almost every new thing I see in the markets, though, and I was, in fact, going to do a chapter in this book on convenience foods, but I've discovered through my testing that they are, on the whole, phony. I do keep piecrust sticks and biscuit mix, and I also use a packaged spaghetti-sauce mix, adding a little red wine to the sauce as it simmers. The sauce is ready in half an hour or so, which gives me the time to make and brown the meat balls and cook the spaghetti. I also adore potato buds, the instant mashed potatoes, for their convenience, and I sometimes resort to instant rice. Those are my major uses for convenience foods.

Besides being full of mysterious ingredients, packaged foods are outrageously expensive.

I now live on an apple orchard, and we barter apples for other fruits and vegetables. To make sure of what I'm talking about, I went out one day and paid 69 cents for a pound of meat and 79 cents for a packaged tamale pie, which my household loves. With tax, that is well over $1.50. Then I bought the real ingredients to make one, as well: 6 cents for the cornmeal (¼ of a 24-cent package); tomato sauce, 11 cents; sliced olives, 11 cents; green pepper, 14 cents; small can of corn, 9 cents; and I'll throw in a few pennies for the chili powder and other seasonings. Including the meat, that's $1.24. And look at what I avoid: dehydrated vegetables, lactose, monosodium glutate, potato starch, citric acid, and a beautiful mysterious ingredient: "imitation flavor." Of what? On another package I have, there is a list of sour-cream solids preserved with BHa and propyl galate in propylene glycate (what's that?), cornstarch, dehydrated vegetables (which?), citric acid, mono- and diglycerides, artificial color, artificial and natural flavors. I have never met a dehydrated vegetable that tasted like a fresh one.

And I have *cheese,* already grated, to put on my tamale pie, because I learned years ago to grate all the ends of hard and semi-hard cheeses and keep them in a screw-top jar in the refrigerator. I might add that my fresh tamale pie takes only a few minutes longer to make than does the packaged mix. And you have to wait in line at the checkout counter just as long for meat and a mix as you do for meat and a few other items.

For your consideration, I offer a quote from George Ade's fable "The Waistband That Was Taut up to the Moment It Gave Way," which is delightful reading for any present-day cook, and can be found in E. B. White and Katharine S. White's *A Subtreasury of American Humor* at any library.

I set a scrumptious Table to the very last.

Moral: Cling to your Ideals, such as they are. I join with Mrs. Stuffer of the above fable. I concur with Mr. Ade's moral as well.

MARGO RIEMAN

Sunset, Utah

1   Springtime

Who wants to cook in the springtime? Let's face it, you have to! Dinners featuring fresh seasonal foods that make it all worthwhile.

COOK-AHEAD DINNERS

CHICKEN BREASTS WITH CHAMPAGNE SAUCE

Serves 4

1 cup chicken broth
Salt
Pepper
Bay leaf

Thyme
1 cup dry white wine or champagne
2 large chicken breasts

1. Preheat oven to 350°.
2. Simmer the chicken broth with the spices for fifteen minutes. Strain, and add wine.
3. Place chicken breasts in a casserole, pour broth over, cover, and bake about fifty-five minutes, or until fork-tender.
4. Strain off broth and reserve. Cool chicken in the casserole and refrigerate.

Sauce

⅔ cup butter
⅓ cup flour
   Remaining chicken broth

2 cups brut *champagne*
1 egg yolk
1 tablespoon cream

1. Preheat oven to 350°.
2. Melt the butter, stir in the flour, and slowly add the chicken broth and champagne, stirring constantly. Cook until thickened.
3. Mix egg yolk with cream, add some of the hot sauce, stirring well, then stir egg-cream mixture into sauce, off the fire. Return to gentle heat, but do not boil.
4. Coat chicken breasts, at room temperature, with some of the sauce and heat in the oven. Serve with the rest of the sauce in a heated sauce boat.

serve with: Melon bites wrapped in prosciutto or Virginia ham, with cocktails, very thin noodles, frozen peas and onions, and Harvey's Little Chocolate Pots (page 86) for dessert.
The wine should be a light, dry white.

CHICKEN KIEV

Serves 4

2 *large chicken breasts, split and*
  boned, pounded very thin by
  butcher
½ *cup butter, at room temperature*
1 *tablespoon chopped parsley*
  Pinch thyme
  Pinch powdered tarragon

1 *teaspoon chopped chives*
  Salt
  Pepper
  Flour for dredging
1 *egg, lightly beaten*
  Fine dry bread crumbs
1 *pint cooking oil*

1. Separate each half breast into two pieces. If the butcher won't do them for you, pound them yourself with any heavy object, between two sheets of waxed paper. Be careful not to pound holes in the breast. You need eight pieces of very thin breast.

2. Cream the butter with the parsley, thyme, tarragon, and chives. Shape into eight small rolls, about 1½ inches long. Chill until very firm.

3. Season the chicken pieces with salt and pepper. Place a piece of the chilled butter in the center of each piece of chicken, and wrap chicken around it, being sure the butter is *entirely* enclosed.

4. Roll each chicken piece in flour, then in beaten egg, then in crumbs. Chill thoroughly until five to ten minutes before serving.

to serve: Heat the oil, about 1 inch deep, to a moderate temperature—370° if you use a deep-fat thermometer. Fry the rolls until moderately golden, about five minutes if you get the chicken very thin. Drain on paper towels and serve immediately.

serve with: Liverwurst spread on sesame crackers with drinks, tomato cups filled with creamed spinach (prepare ahead for last-minute broiling), marinated artichoke hearts on endive-and-lettuce salad, and Black Russians (page 90) for dessert.

The wine should be a Riesling or a Zinfandel.

COQ AU VIN

Serves 4

½ cup butter	1½ cups dry red wine, such as
4 chicken legs and thighs,	Burgundy
separated	1 tablespoon minced parsley
2 chicken breasts, split	1 bay leaf
Flour for dredging	½ teaspoon chives
Salt	½ teaspoon tarragon
Pepper	½ teaspoon thyme
⅛ pound salt pork, diced	3 tablespoons flour
12 mushrooms, sliced	¾ cup water
A small can white onions, drained	¼ teaspoon Kitchen Bouquet

1. Heat butter in a casserole. Shake chicken pieces in flour seasoned with salt and pepper. Sauté chicken in the butter until golden on all sides and remove to a plate. Sauté diced salt pork in the butter until crisp, then add mushrooms and onions and sauté quickly, stirring to brown on all sides.

2. Put chicken on top of mushrooms and onions, add wine, and simmer for thirty minutes. Add parsley and herbs, and simmer forty minutes more, until chicken is tender. Cool and refrigerate, covered, until one hour before serving.

to serve: Bring casserole to room temperature and place on slow fire until simmering gently. Stir flour into water until smooth, add Kitchen Bouquet, and strain through a fine sieve into casserole, stirring well to incorporate. Let simmer until sauce thickens slightly, spooning the sauce over the chicken occasionally, then serve.

serve with: Anchovy Toast Fingers (page 70) with drinks, brown rice, French bread, cold asparagus marinated in Italian dressing, and Chocolate Custard (page 86) for dessert.

The wine should be the same red Burgundy you used for the chicken.

STUFFED PORK CHOPS

Serves 4

4 *double loin pork chops with large*
  pockets cut in by the butcher
Salt
Pepper
2 *cups fine dry bread crumbs*
1 *large onion, minced*

2 *tart apples, peeled, cored, and*
  minced
1 *teaspoon poultry seasoning*
½ *cup chopped pecans*
½ *to 1 cup light cream*

1. Preheat oven to 350°.
2. Season the chops inside and out with salt and pepper.
3. Mix bread crumbs, onion, apples, poultry seasoning, and pecans. Moisten with the cream, taste, and add salt and pepper if needed. Stuff the chops and fasten chop edges together with toothpicks.
4. Heat heavy iron skillet, grease with a little fat cut from a chop edge, and sear chops on both sides.
5. Transfer to a casserole, pile any extra stuffing on top, and cover. Bake for one and a half hours, basting several times with more cream.
6. Cool to room temperature and refrigerate, covered.

to serve: Bring casserole to room temperature and heat in a 350° oven, adding a little more cream, until browned and ready to serve.

serve with: Roquefort-stuffed celery bites with drinks, broccoli with butter and lemon juice, and fresh pineapple for dessert.
   The wine should be a chilled rosé.

VEAL CHOPS ITALIANO

Serves 2

Flour for dredging
Salt
Pepper
4 *veal kidney chops, 1 inch thick*
  (ask your butcher for them in
  advance)
2 *tablespoons butter*

1 *tablespoon olive oil (no*
  substitutes)
1 *medium white onion, peeled*
  and stuck with 2 cloves
1 *teaspoon chopped parsley*
¾ *cup dry white wine*

1. Preheat oven to 350°.

2. Mix flour, salt, and pepper together and dredge chops on each side.

3. Melt butter with oil in a heavy casserole that can be covered and put in the oven. Sauté the chops until golden brown on both sides.

4. Add onion and parsley to pan, then pour in wine. Cover and bake for half an hour, until chops are almost tender.

5. Cool casserole, then refrigerate.

to serve: Bring casserole to room temperature and bake in a 350° oven for another fifteen to twenty minutes.

serve with: Antipasto of salami, pimento, rolled anchovies, artichoke hearts marinated in Italian dressing, olives, and bread sticks. Serve veal with buttered noodles and frozen Italian green beans with toasted slivered almonds. For dessert, biscuit tortoni.

The wine should be an Orvieto or a Soave.

VEAL PAPRIKA

Serves 4

2 *pounds veal cut from the leg and pounded thin by the butcher*
Salt
Pepper
2 *onions, chopped fine*
2 *tablespoons butter*

1 *tablespoon imported Hungarian paprika*
A 10-ounce can chicken broth or 10 ounces dry white wine or a mixture of both
1 *cup sour cream*

1. Trim all fat off the veal. If you haven't been able to get the veal pounded thin by the butcher, pound well with the edge of a saucer. Cut into 1½-inch squares and sprinkle with salt and pepper.

2. Sauté the onions in butter until golden, then add the meat and let it brown slightly over a medium flame. Be sure the onions don't burn. Stir in the paprika.

3. Add chicken broth or wine or mixture to cover and simmer, gently, uncovered, until veal is tender and most of the liquid has disappeared.

4. Cover after cooling and refrigerate.

to serve: Bring pan to room temperature and heat gently over a low flame.

Turn off the flame and let the veal cool slightly, so the sour cream will not curdle when added. Add the sour cream and continue heating, stirring, until the cream is heated through. Do not let it boil.

serve with: Mushroom-Parsley Rolls (page 70) with drinks, broccoli sprinkled with shredded Parmesan cheese, noodles, and a Chocolate Rum Roll (page 87) for dessert.
The wine should be a chilled Chablis.

My first trip to Paris was in April, 1951. It was *almost* totally disastrous. There was a constant cold rain. Parisian taxi drivers were the rudest I'd seen. We couldn't find the things we'd been told to go see, like the Bird Market and the Flea Market or even Les Halles. Notoriously cheerful, I cried a lot from sheer disappointment. But one day, on one of those vain expeditions to find something, we stumbled onto a small restaurant, all wooden walls, big glowing fireplace, shining brass pots, and heavenly smells. The waiter was kind and tried to understand us. And he brought us the following dish, which I have somewhat modified, and which took all the curse off Paris. I wound up in the kitchen with the chef, who showed us (mostly in pantomime) how to make this.

PARISIAN VEAL STEW

Serves 4

2½ pounds veal for stew, cut in
    1-inch cubes
¼ cup flour
½ teaspoon salt
¼ teaspoon coarsely ground
    black pepper
¼ cup olive oil
1 teaspoon imported paprika

½ cup chopped white part of
    scallions
1 teaspoon rosemary
1½ cups dry white wine
8 small white onions
1 tablespoon butter
4 small carrots, scrubbed
1 package frozen peas

1. Put veal, flour, salt, and pepper in a paper bag and shake until veal cubes are coated and covered with the seasoned flour.

2. Heat the oil in a heavy casserole and add the meat. Stir with a wooden spoon, sprinkle with paprika, and cook until well browned on all sides. Add chopped scallions, rosemary, and white wine. Cover casserole and let simmer over low heat for one hour.

3. Peel the small onions and put them in a small saucepan with the butter; add water to cover. Cover pan and let cook gently for twenty minutes. Drain and set aside. Put the onions, covered, and the casserole, cooled, into the refrigerator.

to serve: While casserole comes to room temperature, slice carrots thin, then add to casserole and let cook very slowly for twenty minutes. Drop in the frozen peas (bang them against the sink to break them up) and let cook ten minutes longer, until veal is tender.

serve with: Hot Stuffed Cheese Balls (page 63) with drinks, packaged noodles with slivered almonds, crusty French bread, Zucchini and Raw Mushroom Salad (page 80), and Pears Poached in Red Wine (page 90) for dessert.

The wine should be a chilled rosé.

QUICK-PREPARATION DINNERS

CHICKEN MAUDIE

Serves 4

½ cup flour	⅛ teaspoon cinnamon
Salt	1 frying chicken, cut up
Pepper	½ stick butter
Imported paprika	1 cup chicken broth
½ teaspoon curry powder	

1. Preheat oven to 350°.

2. Mix flour, salt, pepper, paprika, curry, and cinnamon in a paper bag. Shake chicken pieces well in the bag to coat. Remove, let dry a little, and shake again.

3. Melt butter in a skillet that can be covered and heated in the oven.

Sauté the chicken until golden all over, turning with a wooden spoon to brown evenly.

4. Remove chicken and place on heated plate. Keep warm under foil. Add seasoned flour remaining in paper bag to juices in skillet, stir quickly, and pour in chicken broth. Stir over low heat until blended and make a sauce.

5. Return chicken to skillet with sauce, cover, and bake for forty-five minutes, until chicken is fork-tender.

serve with: Smoked salmon on black pumpernickel squares with drinks, instant wheat pilaf, and a salad of orange segments and red onion rings drizzled with olive oil and sprinkled with coarsely ground black pepper. For dessert, pears with Port Salut cheese.

The wine should be a Grenache rosé or a sparkling Portuguese rosé.

TARRAGON CHICKEN WITH GRAPES

Serves 4

2 *large whole chicken breasts, split in half*

1½ *cups dry white wine*

¼ *teaspoon tarragon*

3 *tablespoons butter*

3 *tablespoons flour*

2 *small cans seedless white grapes, drained*

Salt

Pepper

Nutmeg

1. In a covered skillet, gently simmer the chicken breasts in wine and tarragon, until tender.

2. Remove chicken to heated serving plate, cover with foil, and keep warm in a slow oven. Save the broth.

3. Melt butter in a small saucepan, stir in flour, and blend, then stir in reserved broth and cook until slightly thickened. Stir in grapes, season with salt, pepper, and nutmeg, cook until sauce is well heated through, and pour over chicken. Serve at once.

serve with: Cream cheese with red caviar on crackers to start with drinks, boiled tiny red new potatoes, Spinach Salad (page 80), apple slices with Liederkranz cheese for dessert.

The wine should be a chilled California Sauvignon Blanc.

FILET MIGNON WITH MUSHROOM SAUCE

Serves 4

½ pound mushrooms, cleaned and
  sliced
3 tablespoons butter
1 tablespoon brandy
1 tablespoon Madeira
1 tablespoon sherry
1 teaspoon flour

¼ cup sweet butter
1 tablespoon Dijon mustard
  Salt
  Four 1-inch-thick slices filet
  mignon
1 tablespoon fresh chives

1. Sauté fresh sliced mushrooms in 3 tablespoons butter for five minutes, stirring. Add brandy and wines, stir to heat through, and ignite. Stir until the flames die down.

2. Sprinkle flour over, stir in the ¼ cup sweet butter and then the mustard. Continue stirring until sauce thickens slightly. Keep warm over a very low flame.

3. Heat a cast-iron skillet very hot and sprinkle in salt. Pan-broil filets four minutes on one side, three minutes on the other, for medium rare.

4. Place on hot plates, add chives to mushroom sauce, spoon sauce over, and serve.

serve with: Frozen shoestring potatoes, broiled tomato halves, sourdough French rolls, and fresh pineapple sprinkled with kirsch for dessert.
The wine should be a robust Burgundy or Bordeaux.

SHRIMP HAWAIIAN

Serves 2

12 raw jumbo shrimp, shelled
  and deveined
¼ cup soy sauce
1 slice fresh ginger, minced (or
  ¼ teaspoon ground ginger)

6 scallions
6 slices bacon, cut in
  half crosswise

1. Put the shrimp in a bowl and mix with the soy sauce and ginger.

2. Slice off the root ends of the scallions, and cut off most of the green,

to make pieces about 5 inches long. Split in half lengthwise.

3. Lay a piece of scallion on each shrimp and wrap with half a slice of bacon, securing bacon with toothpick to hold in place.

4. Broil under high heat 3 inches from flame for eight or ten minutes, turning once and basting with the soy sauce. Cook until shrimp are pink and bacon is crisp. Baste again with soy sauce just before serving.

serve with: Raw vegetable bites with a sour-cream garlic dip with drinks, hot fluffy rice, salad of avocado and orange slices with bottled Tahitian dressing, chutney with the shrimp, and raspberry sherbet for dessert.

The wine should be a cold, dry white—a Riesling, perhaps.

STEAK DIANE

Serves 4

Salt	*1 teaspoon dry mustard*
4 filet mignon steaks,	*5 teaspoons Worcestershire sauce*
1 inch thick	*¼ cup minced chives*
½ cup butter	*4 ounces brandy*
Pepper	

1. Use a chafing dish or an electric frying pan for this dish. Shortly before serving time, place it on the dining table to heat. Back in the kitchen, sprinkle a little salt over a very hot heavy cast-iron skillet and sear the steaks quickly on both sides to seal in the juices. Transfer them to a *hot* plate and rush them to the table.

2. At the table, add the butter to one side of the pan. When butter is melted, tilt the dish and add the other ingredients except for the brandy. Taste and add more salt if needed. Stir with a fork to blend, then use a spoon to work sauce over steaks.

3. Add brandy, let it heat for a moment, then light it with a match. As it burns, spoon sauce over the steaks until flames die down. Serve at once, on hot plates.

serve with: Ice-cold shrimp with a cocktail dip with drinks, frozen potato patties, mixed green salad with Classic French Dressing (page 76) and Roquefort crumbled over, and a lime sherbet for dessert.

The wine should be a good Burgundy or Zinfandel, red and robust.

VEAL SCALOPPINE MILANO

Serves 2

1 clove garlic
½ cup fine dry bread crumbs
¼ cup minced chives
½ to ¾ pound veal scaloppine
  Flour for dredging
1 beaten egg

¼ cup butter
¼ pound mushrooms, sliced
¼ cup olive oil
  Salt
  Pepper
½ cup Marsala or dry sherry

1. Grate garlic into bread crumbs, add chives, and mix well.

2. Dip scaloppine into flour, then egg, then bread crumbs, then egg again and bread crumbs once more. Set aside on waxed paper to dry out a bit.

3. Melt butter in frying pan over moderate heat and sauté mushrooms quickly. (Mushrooms cooked quickly retain their juices.) Remove mushrooms.

4. Add oil and sauté veal until just golden on each side, about three minutes per side. Do not overcook.

5. Sprinkle with salt and pepper, then pour Marsala or sherry into pan at one side and swirl around. Place scaloppine on hot serving platter, stir wine to gather up all pan juices, and pour over.

serve with: Italian antipasto with drinks, spinach noodles with grated Parmesan or Romano cheese, mixed green salad with Gin Dressing (page 78), espresso coffee. For dessert, spumoni or biscuit tortoni.

The wine should be a light Italian white, such as a Soave or Verdicchio.

2 Summer

It's too hot to cook much, so here are dinners that don't cook *you,* or stifle your guests.

COOK-AHEAD DINNERS

BEEF IN ASPIC

Serves 4

8 slices rare roast beef (from
   delicatessen), ¼ inch thick
   Salt and pepper
   Thyme
   Two 10-ounce cans beef bouillon
2 envelopes unflavored gelatin

1 teaspoon Worcestershire sauce
2 dashes Tabasco
2 cooked carrots, sliced
½ green pepper, cut into thin
   strips
1 bunch watercress

1. Overlap slices of roast beef in a shallow serving dish. Season with salt, pepper, and dried thyme.

2. Make aspic by heating bouillon with 1½ cans water. Soak gelatin in ½ cup cold water for five minutes, then add to warm bouillon, off the flame. Stir to dissolve, adding Worcestershire sauce and Tabasco.

3. Pour aspic over beef slices in serving dish. Garnish with carrot slices and strips of green pepper. Chill and keep refrigerated under plastic wrap.

to serve: Garnish serving dish with sprigs of watercress.

serve with: Almond Cheese Balls (page 64) with drinks, pickled beet slices with onion on lettuce, hot garlic bread, and a frozen fruit cheese-cake (defrosted) for dessert.

The wine should be a chilled rosé.

BLANQUETTE DE VEAU

Serves 4

2 pounds veal, cut for stew
2 stalks celery
1 bay leaf
8 peppercorns
1 clove garlic
½ teaspoon thyme
8 small carrots, cut in 2-inch bits
12 small, peeled boiling onions

2 tablespoons butter
2 tablespoons flour
½ cup plus 2 tablespoons light
   cream
1 egg yolk, beaten
½ pound mushrooms
2 tablespoons lemon juice
   Chopped parsley

1. In a large pan, cover veal with cold water, bring to a boil, and cook five minutes. Discard water and cover again with fresh cold water. Add celery, bay leaf, peppercorns, garlic and thyme and cook slowly over low heat for one hour. Add carrots and onions and continue cooking until meat is tender.

2. Remove meat, carrots, and onions with a slotted spoon, put them in covered dish, and refrigerate. Reduce cooking liquid by boiling over a high fire until there are 1½ cups left, then pour through a strainer into a clean casserole.

3. In a small pan, melt butter, stir in flour, and let cook a minute or two. Add ½ cup cream, all at once, and stir until thickened and smooth. Add 2 tablespoons of this mixture to beaten egg yolk, then carefully stir this mixture back into cream sauce and blend. When well combined, add to reduced cooking liquid, stirring over very low heat, until thickened. Do not let it boil.

4. Cook mushroom caps in ½ cup salted water with lemon juice for five minutes. Add mushrooms to meat and vegetables in the refrigerator, and add mushroom liquid to sauce in the casserole. When sauce is cool, float 2 tablespoons cream over it, then cover and refrigerate.

to serve: Stir sauce well, arrange meat and vegetables in the casserole, and bring just to a simmer. Do not let boil. Sprinkle with chopped parsley just before serving.

serve with: Shrimp Pâté (page 68) with drinks, instant rice, raw spinach and watercress salad with bottled Thousand Island dressing. Rhea's Fruit Dessert (page 88) is the perfect ending.

The wine should be a Riesling if you prefer white, or a red Châteauneuf-du-Pape if you like a soft, flavorful red.

TAHITIAN CHICKEN

Serves 2

3 tablespoons butter
Flour
1 large chicken breast, boned
  and halved
1 bunch washed fresh spinach
  Two 12-inch squares heavy
  aluminum foil
½ small onion, minced fine

1 small clove garlic, minced fine
¼ cup dry white wine
2 teaspoons soy sauce
4 mushrooms, caps and stems,
  sliced
Salt
Pepper
Ground ginger

1. Melt the butter in a skillet, lightly flour the chicken pieces, and brown in the butter on both sides.

2. Discard the stems from 12 or 16 large spinach leaves. Place 6 or 8 leaves on each foil square.

3. Place browned chicken breasts on foil squares. Mix onion, garlic, wine, soy sauce, and mushrooms and spread half over each half chicken breast. Season with salt, pepper, and a pinch of ginger.

4. Cover each half breast with 4 to 6 more spinach leaves and fold foil to make sealed packages. Refrigerate.

to serve: Bring to room temperature and bake one hour in a 350° oven. The foil packages are to be opened at the table.

serve with: Pickled Shrimp (page 67) to go with drinks to start, buttered rice, a salad of avocado and orange slices with Classic French Dressing (page 76), and dessert of coffee ice cream sprinkled with toasted coconut and Kahlúa.

To drink: cold imported beer.

SESAME CHICKEN

Serves 4

2 chicken breasts, split
4 chicken legs and thighs,
　separated
　Salt
　Pepper
2 egg yolks

4 tablespoons honey
1 large clove garlic, crushed
¼ cup soy sauce
¼ cup butter
¼ cup sesame seeds

1. Preheat oven to 350°.
2. Skin chicken pieces and sprinkle them with salt and pepper.
3. Mix together egg yolks, honey, garlic, and soy sauce in pie pan.
4. Roll chicken pieces in mixture and place in buttered baking dish with a lid. Dot generously with butter, sprinkle with sesame seeds, and bake, covered, until just barely tender, about forty-five minutes.
5. Cool to room temperature and refrigerate.

to serve: Bring dish to room temperature and bake in a 350° oven until chicken is fork-tender, about another twenty minutes.

serve with: Rumaki (page 67) with drinks, fluffy white rice with minced parsley, Avocado and Grapefruit Salad (page 77), Peaches in Champagne (page 90) for dessert.

The wine should be a chilled dry California Sauterne.

CURRY OF SHRIMP À LA OPTIMIST

Serves 4

1½ cups raw shrimp, in the shell
　2 cups rich milk or light cream
　1 medium onion, chopped fine
　1 medium tart apple, chopped fine
　2 tablespoons butter
　　Pinch thyme

　Small bay leaf, crushed
　Pinch mace
2 tablespoons imported curry
　powder
1½ tablespoons flour

1. Shell the raw shrimp and soak the shells in the milk or cream for at least an hour. Refrigerate the shrimp.

2. Sauté the onion and apple gently in the butter until limp. Mash them thoroughly with a wooden spoon, then add herbs and curry powder and flour. Cook gently a few minutes more.

3. Add the strained milk or cream (discard shells) and cook, stirring constantly, until smooth and about the consistency of heavy cream. Cool to room temperature and refrigerate.

to serve: Bring both shrimp and sauce to room temperature. Heat sauce over a low flame, then add the shrimp and cook until the shrimp are just pink throughout. Ladle over hot fluffy white rice and serve at once.

serve with: Mushrooms Stuffed with Camembert and Almonds (page 65) with drinks, small dishes of chutney, shredded coconut, slivered orange peel, and finely minced chives. A salad of avocado halves filled with Tart French Dressing (page 76) is good with this, and serve a Strawberry Cream-Cheese Heart (page 89) for dessert.

The wine should be a sparkling rosé.

LAMB SHISH KEBABS

Serves 2

1 medium onion, minced
½ teaspoon salt
¼ cup dry sherry
¼ cup olive oil (no
  substitutes)
1 clove garlic, crushed
2 tablespoons oregano

1 pound boneless lamb shoulder,
  cut into 1½-inch squares
2 green peppers, cut into 1½-inch
  squares
4 to 6 fresh mushrooms
6 to 8 cherry tomatoes

1. Crush the onion with salt in a bowl, then stir in sherry, oil, garlic, and oregano leaves, powdered between your palms over the bowl.

2. Add lamb, stirring well to coat all over. Marinate overnight.

to serve: Thread two long skewers with alternating pieces of pepper, lamb, mushroom, and tomato, until four pieces of lamb are on each skewer. Broil 4 inches from high flame for eight minutes on first side. Turn carefully and broil six minutes more.

serve with: Packaged avocado dip and tortilla chips with cocktails, cracked wheat or brown rice, and cold cooked peas and carrots dressed with mayonnaise. Frozen cheesecake (defrosted) for dessert with instant Turkish or espresso coffee.

The wine: a robust red—Burgundy or Pinot Noir.

MARIN SEAFOOD QUICHE

Serves 6

An 8-ounce package frozen crab
meat, thawed
2 cups cooked fresh shrimp, shelled
and deveined
An 8-ounce package natural Swiss
cheese, chopped
½ cup celery, finely chopped

½ cup scallions, finely chopped
Two 9-inch frozen pie shells
1 cup mayonnaise
¼ cup flour
4 slightly beaten eggs
1 cup dry white wine

1. Preheat oven to 400°.

2. Combine crab, shrimp, cheese, celery, and scallions. Scatter into pie shells.

3. Combine mayonnaise, flour, eggs, and wine and pour over seafood in pie shells.

4. Bake for thirty-five to forty minutes, until a silver knife inserted in center comes out clean. Cool, cover with foil or plastic wrap, and refrigerate.

to serve: Bring pies to room temperature, and reheat in a 300° oven for fifteen to twenty minutes, until heated through. Cut in wedges to serve.

serve with: Deviled eggs to start with drinks; mixed green salad with onion rings, artichoke slices, and orange slices; crisp Italian bread sticks.

The wine should be a dry California Sauterne.

COLD POACHED SALMON

Serves 4

½ cup dry white wine
½ large carrot, in chunks
½ large onion, in chunks
2 cloves
4 peppercorns
1 bay leaf
1 stalk celery, including leaves and
tops, coarsely chopped

1 teaspoon salt
¼ cup chopped fresh parsley
Fish bones and trimmings, if
your fish market has them
4 slices center-cut salmon,
in 1-inch slices
Cheesecloth
1 bunch watercress, for garnish

1. In a pot large enough to hold the fish, put 2 quarts water and the wine and all vegetables and seasonings, including fish trimmings if you can get them. Bring to a boil and simmer ten minutes.

2. Set the fish slices side by side to make one large piece on a big double square of cheesecloth. Tie the ends of the cheesecloth in a loose knot to hold the piece together. Place fish in gently simmering broth, knot on top, and cook at a very slow simmer for ten minutes per pound of fish.

3. Use tongs to remove cheesecloth bag by the knot, and let cool on a serving dish. When cool, unwrap cheesecloth, scrape skin carefully off fish slices, and discard cheesecloth, skin, and broth. Arrange skinned salmon on serving dish, cover with plastic, and refrigerate.

to serve: Remove plastic, garnish serving dish with watercress sprigs, and serve.

serve with: Brandied Pâté (page 63) and rye-bread rounds with drinks, lemon wedges and little bowls of mayonnaise for the salmon, Spinach Salad (page 80), and a platter of mixed fresh fruit (as many kinds as you can find) for dessert.

The wine should be a chilled Chablis or Rhine.

STEAK AND LOBSTER

Serves 2

2 *large lobster tails, thawed*
  and shelled
2 *small filet mignons, 1 to 1½*
  inches thick

2 *large mushrooms*
  Béarnaise sauce, bottled or
  canned

Wrap a lobster tail around the outside of each filet, fastening in place with a metal skewer. Broil over charcoal for five to eight minutes, turning once, or under high flame in broiler for seven to eight minutes.

to serve: Serve with a sautéed mushroom on the end of each skewer, and with Béarnaise sauce in separate small bowls.

serve with: Cream-Cheese Cubes with Soy Sauce and Sesame Seeds (page 71) with drinks, instant mashed potatoes mixed with egg yolks and grated cheese, a salad of firm tomatoes sliced and sprinkled with basil leaves, olive oil, and coarsely ground pepper. Dessert should be Peaches in Champagne (page 90), with espresso coffee afterward.

Brut champagne can be served throughout the meal.

VITELLO TONNATO

Serves 6

1 *cup olive oil*
1 *large carrot, chopped*
2 *large cloves garlic, crushed*
4 *celery stalks, chopped*
1 *teaspoon salt*
1 *teaspoon pepper*
1 *teaspoon basil*
¼ *cup minced parsley*
½ *teaspoon oregano*
2 *whole cloves*

1 *medium onion, chopped*
3½ *pounds boneless leg or rump of*
  veal, rolled and tied by the
  butcher
  A 2-ounce can flat anchovy
  fillets
  Two 7-ounce cans tuna
1 *cup dry white wine*
2 *egg yolks*

1. Put half the olive oil in a big pot and add all other ingredients except

egg yolks. Add enough water to cover the veal, cover, and bring slowly to a boil. Cook slowly for three hours, or until veal is tender.

2. Remove from heat and let the meat cool in its own broth. When cool, remove to a carving surface.

3. Put broth into a blender, or force through a sieve. Beat egg yolks and add remaining ½ cup olive oil drop by drop, beating to incorporate. When this thickens, add puréed broth. Mix well to make a smooth sauce.

4. Remove strings from meat and carve into thin slices. Place on a deep serving platter. Set aside one cup of the sauce and pour the rest over the meat. Cover loosely with foil and refrigerate overnight. Cover the extra sauce and refrigerate also.

to serve: Bring to table.

serve with: Pickled Vegetables (page 66) with drinks, Rice Salad (page 77), Italian bread sticks and sweet butter, and cantaloupe halves filled with port.

The wine should be a dry Italian white.

QUICK-PREPARATION DINNERS

SAN FRANCISCO CAESAR SALAD

Serves 4

2 cloves garlic
1 cup olive oil (no substitutes)
¼ teaspoon dry mustard
¼ teaspoon pepper
A 2-ounce can flat anchovy fillets, drained

2 heads romaine, washed and crisped
1 egg, coddled 1 minute in simmering water
1 cup garlic croutons
½ cup freshly grated Parmesan cheese

1. Crush garlic in salad bowl. Add olive oil, mustard, and pepper and stir well.

2. Add anchovies and crush into dressing with a fork, blending well.

3. Tear romaine into bite-sized pieces and add to salad bowl, and toss to mix with dressing. Add egg and continue to toss until all lettuce is smoothly coated.

4. Sprinkle garlic croutons over salad, add cheese, and toss again at table before serving.

serve with: Black pumpernickel squares with smoked salmon with cocktails, fresh bread sticks, and a big platter of assorted fresh fruit bites for dessert.

To drink: Mexican beer. Carta Blanca, Mexicali, or Moctezuma Dos Equis, a black beer.

CHINESE SHRIMP AND EGGS

Serves 4

Sauce

2 cans chicken consommé
⅛ teaspoon monosodium glutamate
3 tablespoons soy sauce

2 tablespoons cornstarch dissolved
   in a little cold water

Pancakes

8 eggs, lightly beaten
6 scallions, chopped with some
   of the green left on
½ cup sliced fresh mushrooms (if
   canned, drained)
1 cup bean sprouts (if canned,
   drained)

½ cup finely chopped celery
2 cans shrimp, 4½ ounces each,
   drained and chopped if whole
   Peanut oil

1. Combine first four ingredients and simmer until thickened and clear. Keep warm over low heat.

2. Combine eggs, vegetables and shrimp and fry in a small amount of peanut oil, using about 1 large tablespoon for each small pancake. Turn to brown on both sides, and keep warm in a slow oven until all are done.

to serve: Serve three or four small cakes with warm sauce poured over.

serve with: Rumaki (page 67) and cherry tomatoes with a sour-cream dip with drinks, Chinese noodles warmed in the oven, Chinese fortune cookies and almond cookies as dessert.

Tea or warmed sake should be served throughout the meal.

BAKED FILLET OF SOLE ITALIANO

Serves 2

2 *large fillets of sole,*
   about 1 pound in all
Flour
Salt
Pepper
3 *tablespoons butter*
A 10-ounce package frozen
chopped spinach

Dash nutmeg
4 *tablespoons dry white wine*
2 *tablespoons mayonnaise*
2 *tablespoons grated Parmesan*
   cheese

1. Dip the fish fillets in flour mixed with salt and pepper and sauté in 2 tablespoons of the butter until golden on each side.

2. While fish is cooking, cook frozen chopped spinach, cut into cubes for quicker thawing, in the rest of the butter. Don't add water. Season with a dash of nutmeg and spread in a buttered flat oven-to-table baking dish.

3. Place cooked fillets on cooked spinach, sprinkle with wine, and spread each fillet with 1 tablespoon mayonnaise. Cover with the cheese and put under the broiler until well heated throughout.

serve with: Cream-Cheese Cubes with Soy Sauce and Sesame Seeds (page 71) with drinks, canned small whole potatoes crisped in butter, tomato slices with basil and olive oil, strawberries with powdered sugar to dip them into for dessert.

The wine should be a chilled dry white.

FILLET OF SOLE MANILA

Serves 4

6 or 7 scallions
1 clove garlic
½ cup peanut oil
2 pounds fillet of sole
⅓ cup soy sauce

½ cup dry sherry
1 tablespoon grated fresh ginger
root
or
½ teaspoon powdered ginger

1. Chop scallions, using all the white and about 3 inches of green tops, and crush garlic into them. Place in a very lightly oiled baking pan suitable for the table. Place fish fillets on top, in a single layer.

2. Combine the rest of the peanut oil, soy sauce, and sherry and pour over the fish.

3. Sprinkle with grated ginger. (Ginger root keeps forever in the freezer, can be grated or sliced frozen, and is infinitely better than powdered.)

4. Broil 3 inches from flame, about fifteen minutes, until fish flakes easily with a fork.

serve with: Heated frozen egg rolls, in 1-inch slices, and Chinese hot mustard for a dip with drinks, hot buttered instant rice, frozen Chinese vegetables, and Chinese fortune cookies and almond cookies for dessert.

The wine should be a chilled dry white.

LOBSTER MARINARA

Serves 2

4 tablespoons olive oil
1 large or 2 small lobsters,
*   split in half*
Salt
Pepper
1 clove crushed garlic

2 tablespoons minced fresh
*   parsley*
½ teaspoon oregano
½ teaspoon basil
A 15-ounce can marinara sauce

1. Heat olive oil in a large skillet and sauté lobster, cut side down, for five minutes.

2. Turn and top with herbs and spices, pouring marinara sauce over at the last.

3. Add water to make liquid to the depth of ¼ inch, cover, and steam for twenty minutes over a low flame.

serve with: Brandied Roquefort Spread (page 66) with drinks, fettucine tossed with melted butter, Italian green beans with slivered almonds (frozen), tomato slices with basil and olive oil. Dessert of Camembert or Liederkranz spread on thin apple slices.

The wine: a sparkling rosé or a dry Orvieto.

SPAGHETTI CARBONARA

Serves 4

1 pound spaghetti	6 slices bacon, diced into
Salt	¼-inch squares
3 beaten eggs	2 tablespoons olive oil
⅓ cup grated Parmesan cheese	Butter
⅓ cup grated Romano cheese	Coarsely ground pepper

1. Slide spaghetti into a *large* pot of salted, boiling water. Cook seven or eight minutes, until *al dente* (which does not mean hard as a tooth, but still just a little firm when you bite it).

2. While spaghetti is cooking, beat eggs, at room temperature, with both grated cheeses.

3. Fry diced bacon in olive oil until crisp. (Yes, cook the bacon in the oil. You want both the bacon-fat flavor and the olive-oil flavor in the finished dish.)

4. Drain spaghetti and place in a very hot, lightly buttered saucepan. Add egg-cheese mixture and very hot bacon-and-oil mixture, season with pepper, and stir rapidly so that egg mixture cooks *onto* hot spaghetti. Serve on hot plates.

serve with: Mushroom-Parsley Rolls (page 70) with drinks, mixed green salad with Classic French Dressing (page 76), lime sherbet with crème de menthe for dessert.

The wine should be a dry Italian white—a Soave or a Verdicchio.

STEAK FRANÇAISE

Serves 2

2 teaspoons black peppercorns,
    coarsely crushed with mortar
    and pestle (or in foil with any
    heavy object)
2 slices filet mignon, 1 inch thick
2 tablespoons butter
1 tablespoon olive oil

1 teaspoon Kitchen Bouquet
1 tablespoon water
4 tablespoons brandy, preferably
    cognac
2 tablespoons very finely minced
    scallion

1. With the heel of your hand, press crushed pepper firmly into both sides of filets. Let sit for ten minutes.

2. Melt butter in heavy frying pan and add oil. Heat until butter stops bubbling.

3. Sauté steaks four minutes on one side, three on the other for rare, five minutes, then four minutes for medium. Add one minute to each side if steaks are thicker. Remove meat to platter in warm oven.

4. Mix Kitchen Bouquet with water and brandy. Add to frying pan, over the fire, stir well, then remove from flame. Add scallions and pour over steaks.

serve with: Chilled madrilene to start dinner, Spinach Salad (page 80), hot garlic-herb bread, and canned heated shoestring potatoes with steaks. Black Russians (page 90) make a marvelous dessert.

The wine should be a robust red Burgundy or a claret.

3 Fall

Fall is a state of mind. These hearty dinners are for those who feel they may die with the leaves and melt in the rain.

COOK-AHEAD DINNERS

CALIFORNIA CHICKEN

Serves 4

½ cup butter
3 or 4 mild Bermuda onions,
   sliced
2 chicken breasts, split
   and boned

2 chicken legs and thighs,
   separated
Salt
Pepper
Pinch tarragon

1. Preheat oven to 300°.

2. Melt half the butter in a large casserole and add sliced onions to make a layer about 1½ inches thick. Over low heat, let onions simmer gently until golden, stirring from time to time.

3. Melt the rest of the butter in a large skillet and brown the chicken parts until golden, about twenty minutes if done in two batches. (If you crowd them, they won't brown.)

4. Lay browned chicken parts on the bed of onions, pour in any butter left over in the skillet, add salt, pepper, and tarragon. Cook, covered, about twenty-five minutes, or until chicken is tender and the onions reduced to a purée.

5. Cool and refrigerate covered overnight.

to serve: Bring casserole to room temperature and reheat in a 350° oven.

serve with: A dip of red caviar and sour cream with drinks, frozen shoe-string potatoes, Zucchini and Raw Mushroom Salad (page 80), hot French bread to dip into the onion sauce, and a lemon pie or sherbet for dessert.
The wine should be a dry white.

I got the chili recipe that follows from a friend in New York. It is one of her contributions to good living, and like her, it swings!

Bette's recipe is very close to the one given by H. Allen Smith in "The Great Chili Confrontation," although he adds the oregano, basil, and cumin I've included here. I go even further, with a truly luxurious variation: I use ground venison, because nothing in the world makes as good chili as that does. Chili is *the* logical thing to make with ground venison; in fact, it is the only thing to do with it. The recipe still makes a marvelous chili with ordinary ground meat. I made it for years using that.

CHILI CON CARNE

Serves 8

¼ pound beef kidney fat
    or suet
1½ pounds ground chuck (or
    ground venison)
 2 small onions, minced fine
 2 cloves garlic, crushed
 4 tablespoons Gebhardt's
    Chili Powder
2½ cups (a 1-pound, 4-ounce
    can) solidpack tomatoes

 1 tablespoon imported paprika
¾ tablespoon salt
    Pinch cayenne
½ teaspoon oregano
¼ teaspoon basil
¼ teaspoon cumin seed or comino
    powder
    Three 1-pound cans red kidney
    beans
Chopped onions for garnish

1. In a heavy enameled-iron skillet, heat fat or suet until melted. Discard membranes, add meat and 1 cup water, and cook uncovered over low heat for half an hour.

2. Stir in onions, garlic, chili powder, and tomatoes. Simmer for an hour. Stir in other spices.

3. Drain two cans of the beans and add, along with the undrained beans. Heat until beans are heated through; then cool and refrigerate, covered.

to serve: Bring casserole or skillet to room temperature, then heat gently, and serve with a bowl of finely chopped raw onion to be sprinkled over.

serve with: Packaged avocado dip and tortilla chips with drinks, soda crackers with the chili, mixed green salad with Classic French Dressing (page 76), and Crème Brûlée (page 85) for dessert.

A Mexican beer (Dos Equis if you can find it, or Carta Blanca) is the only possible beverage with this meal.

Cioppino is a uniquely San Francisco dish. It is pronounced *chaw-PEE-no,* and there are many versions of how it came about. I like best the one that has the Italian fishermen bringing their catch home to the wharf in the evenings, to be cooked in a large pot of tomato-flavored sauce their wives had been preparing. And the wives would go from boat to boat, saying, "Cheep in" for contributions to the pot.

CIOPPINO

Serves 4

1 *dozen clams in the shell, scrubbed*	¼ *pound peeled raw shrimp*
1 *large onion, finely chopped*	1 *pound red snapper fillets*
¼ *teaspoon marjoram*	*A 1-pound can Italian plum tomatoes*
¼ *teaspoon rosemary*	*A 6-ounce can tomato paste*
¼ *teaspoon sage*	½ *cup olive oil*
¼ *teaspoon thyme*	*Salt to taste*
2 *teaspoons sweet basil*	½ *teaspoon black pepper*
2 *tablespoons parsley*	2 *tablespoons La Victoria green and yellow chili salsa or 2 small red peppers*
2 *large cloves garlic, crushed*	
2 *cups coarsely chopped Swiss chard*	½ *cup dry sherry and dry California Sauterne, mixed*
1 *large cracked crab or two medium ones*	

1. Place scrubbed clams in the bottom of a 6- to 8-quart kettle. Mix onions, herbs, and chard and place a layer over clams. Add cracked crab and another layer of herb mix.

2. Add shrimp and remaining herb mix. Place snapper fillets on top.

3. Mix tomatoes, tomato paste, olive oil, salt, pepper, and chili salsa in 1 quart hot water, and add to kettle. Cover and simmer thirty minutes. Cool and refrigerate.

to serve: Bring kettle to room temperature, add wine mix, and simmer ten more minutes, or until blended. Serve in large soup bowls.

serve with: Celery bites stuffed with deviled ham with drinks, crusty French bread, mixed green salad, fruit and cheese for dessert.

The wine should be a California Sauterne.

LASAGNA

Serves 6

¼ cup olive oil
½ pound ground beef
½ pound Italian sweet
    sausage
    Two 10-ounce cans Italian
    meat sauce
 1 tablespoon salt
½ pound lasagna noodles

2 eggs
2 cups ricotta or cottage
    cheese
¼ cup chopped parsley
    Two 10-ounce packages
    mozzarella
½ cup grated Parmesan cheese

1. Heat 2 tablespoons of the oil in a skillet, then add the beef and skinned sausage. Cook, stirring to break up into chunks, until done through. Add meat sauce, bring to a simmer, and let cook gently.

2. In a large pot, put 6 to 8 cups of water to boil. When boiling hard, add salt and 2 tablespoons oil, then carefully slide the noodles in, one at a time, letting them soften and bend. Boil gently for ten to fifteen minutes, until fork-tender.

3. While noodles are cooking, break eggs into a bowl, add ricotta or cottage cheese and parsley and mix thoroughly. Cut mozzarella into pieces the size of a quarter and set aside.

4. When noodles are done, drain and cover with warm water.

5. To assemble: Oil a 9 x 12 x 3 baking pan. Lift the noodles, one at a time, across your palms out of the warm water and lay them crosswise in the pan, with the ends extending up the sides. Spread a *thin* layer of meat sauce over the noodles, spreading it with a spatula, then spread a thin layer of the egg-cheese mixture over. Sprinkle lightly with Parmesan and dot with mozzarella. Repeat the layerings, ending with Parmesan and mozzarella. Cover and refrigerate.

to serve: Bring pan to room temperature and bake thirty to forty minutes in a 350° oven. Let stand for ten to fifteen minutes to set before cutting into squares to serve.

serve with: Shrimps with Anchovy Butter (page 68) with drinks, a mixed green salad, and a fruit compote for dessert.
The wine should be a Chianti, red and robust.

MEATBALLS AND EGGPLANT ARNONE

Serves 4 to 6

1½ pounds ground chuck
¾ cup Italian seasoned bread
    crumbs
1 small onion, minced fine
¼ cup grated Parmesan cheese
¾ teaspoon cornstarch
    Pinch ground allspice
    Pinch mace
1 egg, slightly beaten
¾ cup light cream

¾ teaspoon salt
    Flour
¼ cup oil, preferably olive oil
1 medium eggplant
¼ teaspoon salt
1 cup salad oil
8 ounces mozzarella, shredded
    Two 15-ounce cans tomato
    sauce
½ teaspoon oregano

1. Mix meat, crumbs, onion, Parmesan, cornstarch, allspice, and mace with egg, cream, and ¾ teaspoon salt. Work this mixture with your hands until smooth, then shape into 2-inch meatballs and roll in flour. Brown, a few at a time, all over in oil, shaking the skillet to turn them. Set aside when all are browned.

2. Slice eggplant into ½-inch slices, salt them, and place them in a bowl under a plate for half an hour. Pour off liquid, flour slices, and sauté in 1 cup salad oil until golden on each side.

3. In a large casserole or bake-and-serve pan, make a layer of eggplant, meatballs, mozzarella, and tomato sauce, using half of each. Repeat for second layer, sprinkle with oregano, then cover with foil and refrigerate.

to serve: Bring casserole to room temperature and bake for one hour at 350°, uncovered. Let stand ten minutes before serving.

serve with: Salami–Cream-Cheese Bites (page 69) with drinks, mixed green salad with a Tart French Dressing (page 76), hot garlic bread, and Zabaglione (page 89) for dessert.

The wine should be a good Chianti or Bardolino.

PORK CHOPS MALAYAN

Serves 2

½ teaspoon salt
 4 pork chops, 1 inch thick
⅔ cup raw long-grain rice
½ cup raisins
½ cup sliced almonds
 2 scallions, minced fine

 4 mushrooms, sliced
½ teaspoon (or more) imported
    Indian curry powder
 1 cup dry white wine
    An 8-ounce can tomato sauce

1. Heat a large heavy skillet that can be covered. Add salt and sear chops until brown on each side.

2. While chops brown, combine rice, raisins, almonds, scallions, mushrooms, and curry powder.

3. Spoon rice mixture around browned chops, pour wine over, and then pour tomato sauce over.

4. Cover, bring to a boil, and then simmer gently for forty-five minutes. Cool and refrigerate, covered.

to serve: Bring skillet to room temperature and pour a little more wine over. Place in a 350° oven until heated through and bubbling gently.

serve with: Deviled Nuts (page 65) with drinks, a salad of thin onion and orange slices drizzled with olive oil and sprinkled with coarsely ground black pepper, and lemon sherbet with a little green crème de menthe poured over.

The wine should be a light dry red, such as a Zinfandel.

PAELLA

Serves 4

 1 onion, chopped
¼ cup olive oil
 8 pieces chicken (legs, thighs,
    and split breasts)
1¼ cups long-grain rice
 1 clove garlic, mashed
 1 tablespoon shredded saffron or
    ⅛ teaspoon powdered saffron

1½ cups chicken broth
 8 shelled raw shrimp
 1 dozen clams in the shell or 1
    small can minced clams
½ package frozen peas
 1 small jar sliced pimento
¼ cup grated Romano or Parmesan
    cheese

1. Preheat oven to 350°.

2. Cook onion in olive oil until golden, remove to plate, and brown chicken parts in the same oil. Remove to plate with onions.

3. Add rice (and a little more oil if necessary) and cook, stirring, until golden and glazed. Combine garlic, saffron and broth; bring to a simmer.

4. In a large casserole, put chicken, onions, broth, and rice. Bake, covered, until rice is tender, about 1½ hours. Add more broth if necessary, but do not stir. Cool and refrigerate.

5. On serving day, place casserole, at room temperature, in 350° oven for fifteen minutes. Poke shrimp and clams down into the paella, or very carefully stir in drained minced clams. Sprinkle peas over and decorate with pimento strips. Sprinkle with cheese. Bake, uncovered, fifteen minutes longer.

serve with: Raw vegetable bites and your favorite sour-cream dip, a mixed green salad, warm crusty French bread, and Irish Coffee (page 91) for dessert.

The wine should be a chilled, very dry white, such as a Chablis.

SWISS STEAK

Serves 4

Salt	1 large onion, thinly sliced
Pepper	1 green pepper, cut in ¼-inch strips
2 pounds round steak, 1½ inches thick	A 1-pound can solidpack tomatoes
¾ cup flour	1 cup (or more) dry red wine
¼ cup oil or shortening	2 to 4 drops Tabasco

1. Preheat oven to 350°.

2. Salt and pepper the steak on both sides, then pound as much flour as possible into each side, using a potato masher or heavy saucer.

3. Heat oil in heavy casserole with lid, add meat, and brown well on each side over high heat.

4. Arrange onions, green peppers, and tomatoes over meat. Add red wine mixed with Tabasco, cover tightly, and bake for one and a half to two hours, until meat is fork-tender. Add a little more wine if the pot gets dry. Cool and refrigerate.

to serve: Bring casserole to room temperature and bake another half hour in a 350° oven. Again, add more wine if pot gets dry.

serve with: Toasted Parmesan Bread Cubes (page 71) with drinks, mixed green salad with Mandarin orange sections and avocado, frozen stuffed baked potatoes, and Chocolate-Wafer–Whipped-Cream Dessert (page 86).
The wine should be a robust red, such as a Pinot Noir.

TURKEY DIVINE

Serves 4 to 6

8 ounces thin spaghetti or linguine
  Salt
¼ cup butter
¼ cup flour
¼ teaspoon nutmeg
2 cups chicken or turkey broth
1 cup light cream
¼ cup dry sherry or Marsala

¼ cup grated Parmesan cheese
2 cups cooked turkey, cubed
¼ cup chopped green pepper
½ pound sliced mushrooms
1 teaspoon minced scallion
1 egg yolk
½ cup slivered almonds

1. Break spaghetti or linguine into 3-inch pieces and drop into 6 cups boiling salted water. Bring to boil again. Stir constantly with a wooden spoon or fork for three minutes. Cover and remove from heat. Let stand for ten minutes and drain. Put into a warm, buttered bowl.

2. Meanwhile, melt butter over low heat, blend in flour, 1 teaspoon salt, and nutmeg, and stir constantly until mixture is smooth and bubbly. Remove from heat, stir in broth and cream, and bring to simmer, stirring for one minute. Add wine and cheese, stirring, then pour over pasta.

3. Add turkey, green pepper, mushrooms, scallion, and egg yolk to spaghetti-sauce dish and mix all together.

4. Pour into buttered baking-serving dish and sprinkle with almonds. Cool, cover with foil, and refrigerate.

to serve: Uncover serving dish and bring to room temperature. Bake uncovered for twenty-five to thirty minutes. Let stand ten minutes before serving.

serve with: Canned warm jalapeño-bean dip with corn chips with drinks,

Spinach and Watercress Salad (page 80), hot butterflake rolls, pineapple sherbet with a sauce of puréed, sweetened frozen raspberries flavored with brandy.

The wine should be a California Sauterne or a dry Riesling.

QUICK-PREPARATION DINNERS

CHICKEN LIVERS VIN ROUGE

Serves 2

1 *pound chicken livers*
2 *tablespoons butter*
2 *medium tomatoes, in chunks*

½ *cup dry red wine*
1 *teaspoon rosemary*

1. Rinse chicken livers, drain on paper towels, and cut each in two pieces.

2. Melt butter in skillet and when bubbling add livers, browning them quickly over a medium-high flame.

3. Add the other ingredients, bring to a boil, and simmer gently until livers are just barely pink in the center—five to seven minutes.

serve with: Garlic-clam dip with drinks, then livers and sauce over hot buttered rice, frozen baby lima beans, and lemon-meringue pie for dessert.

The wine can be the same dry red used to cook the livers—a Beaujolais is perfect.

FESTIVE HAM SLICES

Serves 4

2 *center-cut ham slices, about*
  1 *inch thick*
2 *cooking apples, unpeeled, sliced*
  ½ *inch thick*
½ *cup orange marmalade*
¼ *teaspoon Worcestershire sauce*

½ *teaspoon dry mustard*
¼ *teaspoon ginger*
2 *drops Tabasco*
4 *tablespoons Grand Marnier or*
  brandy

1. Preheat oven to 350°.

2. Slash the fat around the edge of each ham slice. Place one in a baking-serving dish, place apple slices over it, and put the other ham slice on top.

3. Mix marmalade, Worcestershire, mustard, ginger, and Tabasco to a paste. Spread over top slice of ham.

4. Bake for about thirty minutes, until glazed and shiny.

5. Warm the Grand Marnier or brandy in a small pan and ignite. Pour flaming over ham and serve while still blazing.

serve with: Vegetable bites and a sour-cream dip with drinks, instant mashed yams, broccoli, and fresh pineapple spears sprinkled lightly with kirsch for dessert.

The wine should be a rosé or a light dry white.

HAM SLICE TOTTEN

Serves 2 or 3

1 *slice precooked ham, center cut,*
  ¾ inch thick
¾ *cup currant jelly*
2 *tablespoons prepared Dijon*
  mustard

2 *tablespoons minced fresh*
  scallion

1. Cut a little piece of fat from the edge of the ham and use it to grease a heavy chafing dish or skillet.

2. Sauté ham slice on one side until it browns lightly, then turn and brown the other side. Place on warm plate in the oven, at 300°.

3. Put jelly, mustard, and minced scallion in the skillet or chafing dish and stir together. When jelly melts and sauce is hot, put ham slice back in pan.

4. Let simmer in sauce for a few moments, turn and simmer a few moments more.

serve with: Canned warm jalapeño-bean dip and tortilla chips with drinks, drained canned golden hominy crisped in butter, broccoli spears with bottled Hollandaise, heat-and-serve butterflake rolls. Frozen or bakery pumpkin pie, warmed and sprinkled with a little bourbon for dessert.

The wine should be a light, dry red, such as a California Zinfandel.

PRAWNS GUADALAJARA

Serves 4

4 small cloves garlic, crushed
4 scallions, white part only, finely
   chopped
1 cup butter at room temperature
3 tablespoons A.1. Sauce
4 dashes Tabasco

2 tablespoons lemon juice
½ teaspoon salt
½ teaspoon coarsely ground black
   pepper
16 large fresh prawns, peeled and
   deveined, tails left on

1. Mix together garlic, scallions, butter, A.1. Sauce, Tabasco, lemon juice, salt and pepper over low heat. Keep warm in a double boiler or in another pan of water. Do not let brown.

2. Split prawns lengthwise, being careful not to cut them clear through. Place the prawns, split sides up, in an oiled baking dish and broil 4 inches from high flame for five minutes.

3. Pour warm butter sauce over shrimp, return to broiler for one minute and serve at once.

serve with: Melon with prosciutto (or boiled ham) bites to start, brown rice mix, French bread, and a salad of tomato slices with olive oil and sprinkled with basil leaves. Assorted cheeses and fruit for dessert.
The wine should be a light dry white.

SALTIMBOCCA

Serves 4

Flour
8 thin slices of veal, cut from the
   leg, pounded thin
8 slices prosciutto (or boiled ham)
4 slices mozzarella
2 cans mushrooms, drained and
   thinly sliced

Salt
Pepper
4 tablespoons olive oil
4 tablespoons butter
¼ cup dry white wine

1. Lightly flour the veal and lay, floured side down, on a work surface. Top four of the veal pieces with a slice of prosciutto (almost to the edge of the veal), then add a slice of cheese. Add mushrooms, a pinch of salt and pepper. Add second slice of ham, then second slice of veal, floured side out.

2. Seal the edges of this "sandwich" with the blunt edge of a knife, by pressing edges of veal together *firmly*.

3. Warm the oil in a large skillet, then add butter. Sauté the meat until the underside is golden, over a low flame, then sprinkle with wine. Turn and brown the other side, basting with the pan juices. The wine will evaporate. Serve with the pan juices poured over.

serve with: Cold shrimp with cocktail sauce to start, fettucine, peas, and Neapolitan ice-cream slices sprinkled with toasted almond slivers.

The wine should be a California Sauterne.

BROILED MARINATED SCALLOPS

Serves 4

½ cup olive oil
½ cup dry vermouth
 2 cloves garlic, crushed
¾ teaspoon salt

2 tablespoons minced parsley
1½ pound scallops, preferably
    fresh

1. Mix together the oil, vermouth, garlic, salt, and parsley. Marinate scallops in this mixture overnight.

2. Arrange the undrained scallops in a shallow oven-to-table dish.

3. Broil 2 inches from heat, turning to brown delicately on all sides.

serve with: Packaged avocado spread and crackers with drinks, packaged herb-seasoned rice, tiny frozen whole green beans, frozen cheesecake for dessert.

The wine should be a dry white, such as a dry California Sauvignon Blanc.

GROUND SIRLOIN FRANÇAISE

Serves 2

1 *pound ground sirloin*
2 *pieces Roquefort cheese, about*
  1 inch square
  Salt
2 *tablespoons butter*
2 *tablespoons finely chopped*
  scallions
2 *tablespoons finely chopped*
  parsley

2 *tablespoons finely chopped*
  green pepper
2 *tablespoons finely chopped basil*
  leaves
¾ *cup dry red wine*
1 *tablespoon Worcestershire*
  sauce

1. Shape meat into two thick cakes around the cheese, making sure the cheese is covered completely.

2. Heat a heavy iron skillet very hot, sprinkle with salt, and sear meat three or four minutes on each side for rare, five or six minutes for medium rare.

3. Remove meat to hot platter and keep warm in oven, under foil.

4. Add butter to pan, add chopped scallions, parsley, green pepper, and basil leaves, and cover pan for two minutes, shaking to stir greens around. Add wine and Worcestershire sauce and heat through, then pour over meat and serve.

serve with: Bottled marinated mushrooms with drinks, Beef Rice-a-Roni, frozen peas and onions, crusty French bread, frozen apple turnover for dessert.

The wine should be a dry red, such as a red Burgundy.

4 Winter

Winter brings the holidays—also snow, sleet,
and blizzards, followed by hungry people.
These are meals to bring comfort and cheer
against the cold.

COOK-AHEAD DINNERS

CARBONNADE OF BEEF

Serves 4

2 pounds round steak, cut in
   1½-inch cubes
2 tablespoons butter
2 medium onions, sliced
   12-ounce can of beer, opened to
   get flat
4 teaspoons cornstarch
2 teaspoons powdered sugar

½ cup beef bouillon (1 cube
   dissolved in ½ cup water)
1 teaspoon salt
¼ teaspoon pepper
   Pinch each of marjoram, thyme,
   and caraway seeds
1 bay leaf
1 tablespoon minced parsley

1. Preheat oven to 300°.
2. Brown meat on all sides in a heavy skillet in a little of its own fat. Remove meat, add butter, and sauté onions until golden.
3. Layer meat and onions in a casserole.
4. Discard fat remaining in skillet, pour in flat beer, and stir.
5. Dissolve cornstarch and sugar in bouillon, pour into skillet and add all seasonings. Bring to a boil, stirring, then pour over meat in casserole. Bake for two hours, until tender. Cool and refrigerate, covered.

to serve: Bring casserole to room temperature, and reheat gently in 350° oven for thirty minutes, until bubbling and sauce is thickened.

serve with: Marinated artichoke hearts and marinated mushrooms with sesame-seed crackers and drinks, then noodles sprinkled with buttered bread crumbs, green salad with tomatoes, cucumbers, chopped green peppers, and scallions. Serve frozen apple turnovers for dessert.
   To drink: an imported Dutch or German beer.

CHICKEN FLORENTINE

Serves 4

1 *3–4-pound roasting chicken*
  Salt
  Pepper
3 *tablespoons dried tarragon leaves*
2 *carrots*
2 *onions*
2 *stalks celery, leaves and all*

3 *sprigs parsley*
2 *tablespoons butter*
2 *tablespoons flour*
1 *cup dry white wine*
2 *egg yolks*
1 *cup light cream*
¼ *cup minced fresh parsley*

1. Wash the chicken inside and out, pat dry with paper towels, and sprinkle inside and out with salt and pepper. Rub inside with 2 tablespoons of the tarragon. Place in a large stewing pot with carrots, onions, celery, cut in pieces. Add parsley. Cover with boiling water, simmer until almost fork-tender, then let cool in pot until tender. Cool the chicken, cover, and refrigerate. Strain off 1 cup of cooking liquid and discard the rest.

2. Melt the butter in a saucepan, stir in the flour to blend, and simmer for a few moments. Then add, all at once, the broth, the wine, and the rest of the tarragon. Let this simmer gently, stirring, until thickened. Meanwhile, mix egg yolks with cream. Cool sauce, then cover and refrigerate both sauce and egg yolk–cream mixture.

to serve: Before serving, remove chicken and skin it. Put, under foil, in a slow oven to warm up while you finish sauce. Heat the wine-broth sauce gently, then add it gradually, a spoonful at a time, to the egg yolk–cream mixture. When well blended, return to a gentle heat but do not let boil. When well thickened, spoon over chicken in a pretty casserole. Garnish with the minced parsley. Take to table and serve.

serve with: Raw cauliflower bites and a sour-cream garlic dip with drinks, boiled tiny red new potatoes, onion and orange slices on lettuce, and Cold Lemon Mold (page 88) for dessert.

The wine should be a very light dry white, such as a Riesling.

CHICKEN FRICASSEE WITH HERB DUMPLINGS

Serves 4

1 4-pound stewing chicken, cut
　into pieces
1 large whole onion
1 large whole carrot
1 stalk celery with leaves
1 bay leaf
12 peppercorns
2 tablespoons butter

2 tablespoons flour
4 carrots, cut in 1-inch slices
　Salt
　Pepper
2 cups unsifted Bisquick
¼ cup minced fresh parsley
¼ teaspoon rosemary
¾ cup milk

1. Put chicken, onion, carrot, celery, bay leaf, and peppercorns into a large pot with enough water to cover. Cook gently for one hour.

2. Remove chicken to a plate, remove skin and loose pieces of bone or gristle and discard.

3. Strain broth in kettle through a sieve, discard seasonings and return clear broth to kettle. With a fork, blend butter and flour well together and add, bit by bit, to the broth, stirring with a whisk to incorporate. Bring broth to a simmer, add sliced carrots, the chicken pieces, and salt and pepper to taste. Cook thirty minutes more. Cover after cooling and refrigerate.

to serve: Bring fricassee to a simmer. Follow directions on the Bisquick package for dumplings, mixing the parsley and rosemary in with the mix before adding the milk. Blend well with a fork, then spoon on top of the simmering fricassee, making eight dumplings in all. Serve immediately after dumplings are cooked.

serve with: Hot Ham Snacks (page 72) with drinks, Zucchini and Mushroom Salad (page 80), and Chocolate Custard (page 86) for dessert.

The wine should be a light, dry white, such as a Pinot Blanc.

LAMB CURRY

Serves 6 to 8

2 lbs. boned lamb shoulder
cut in 1-inch cubes
¼ cup flour
6 tablespoons butter
2 tablespoons imported Indian
curry powder
2 cups chicken broth
2 bay leaves
1 stick whole cinnamon
3 whole cloves
1 teaspoon salt
¼ teaspoon turmeric
½ teaspoon pepper

½ teaspoon ground cumin
½ teaspoon ground cardamom
2 teaspoons imported paprika
4 pearl onions, peeled
½ cup white raisins
½ cup shelled pine nuts (go to
an Italian store)
¼ teaspoon grated lemon peel
1 slice (size of a quarter) fresh
ginger, minced
1 green pepper, in 1-inch squares
1 tomato, cut in 8 pieces
1 green winter pear

1. Coat meat cubes in flour, then sauté in 4 tablespoons butter in large casserole. In another pan, sauté curry powder in 2 tablespoons butter and add chicken broth and all nine spices. Simmer for two minutes, then pour over meat.

2. Add all other ingredients except pear and cook over medium heat for two hours, or until lamb is tender. Fish out cinnamon stick (if possible), cool, cover, and refrigerate.

to serve: Bring casserole to room temperature and place over moderate flame. Peel and core the pear, slice it into 8 pieces, add to curry and let cook ten minutes more.

serve with: Deviled Nuts (page 65) with drinks, then lots of fluffy white rice, condiments in separate bowls: Sun Brand Chutney, chopped hard-boiled eggs, shredded coconut, chopped cashews, watermelon pickles. The salad is thin slices of orange and onion, drizzled with olive oil and sprinkled with coarse black pepper. Lemon sherbet for dessert.

To drink: cold, imported Dutch beer.

BAKED BASQUE LAMB

Serves 4

2 pounds ground lamb
1 medium onion, chopped
1 clove garlic, crushed
¼ cup fresh parsley, chopped
   fine with scissors
½ teaspoon salt

¼ teaspoon pepper
2 tablespoons butter
   A 16-ounce can tomatoes
   (2 cups)
½ cup lemon juice
2 drops Tabasco

1. Preheat oven to 350°.

2. Mix lamb, onion, garlic, parsley, salt, and pepper. Spread in a baking dish suitable for the table.

3. Top with small dots of butter and bake for thirty minutes.

4. Spread tomatoes over and bake another thirty minutes. Cool and refrigerate under foil.

to serve: Bring baking dish to room temperature and heat for five minutes in a 350° oven. Mix lemon juice with Tabasco and pour over, and bake five minutes more, or until thoroughly heated.

serve with: Black bread squares with pimento and anchovy strips with drinks, frozen French fries, mixed green salad with Vinaigrette Dressing (page 79), apples and cheese or apple pie for dessert.

The wine should be a Burgundy or a Pinot Noir.

ITALIAN VEAL SHANKS IN WHITE WINE

Serves 4

¼ cup flour
½ teaspoon salt
¼ teaspoon pepper
   Veal shank, cut in 3-inch
   lengths (2 per person)
¼ cup olive oil (no substitute)

½ teaspoon paprika
2 cups dry white wine
2 cloves garlic, crushed
2 strips lemon peel
1 teaspoon basil

1. Mix flour, salt, and pepper in a paper bag, add veal shanks, and shake to coat well.

2. Heat olive oil in casserole and brown shanks well on all sides.

3. Add all other ingredients, cover and simmer gently for one hour, or until veal is almost falling off the bones.

4. Cool, and refrigerate, covered.

to serve: Bring casserole to room temperature and simmer gently for about twenty minutes. Remove meat, keep warm, and cook sauce left in casserole until slightly thickened, then pour over meat and serve.

serve with: Cheese Sticks (page 64) with drinks, buttered noodles, mixed green salad with marinated artichoke hearts and Vinaigrette Dressing (page 79), and garlic bread. For dessert serve pear and apple slices to be spread with Liederkranz and/or Camembert cheese. Espresso coffee goes well, too.

The wine should be the same dry white you used with the meat.

PORK CHOPS BORRACHO

Serves 4

8 pork chops	1 package frozen baby lima beans
Flour	1 teaspoon thyme
Salt	Pinch of sage
Pepper	1 cup hard cider
1 medium onion, sliced thin	½ cup applejack or Calvados

1. Preheat oven to 350°.

2. Heat a large heavy skillet and rub with the fat edge of one chop to grease. Dip chops in flour seasoned with salt and pepper. Sauté until lightly browned on both sides.

3. Transfer chops to baking-serving dish and cover with onion slices and frozen baby limas. (Whack package of limas against sink to loosen.) Season with thyme and sage.

4. Rinse out skillet with cider, scraping with a wooden spoon to get the brown bits, then pour over chops. Cover pan with foil and bake one hour, adding more cider if pan gets dry. Cool and refrigerate, covered.

to serve: Bring pan to room temperature, pour the applejack or Calvados over the chops, and reheat for fifteen minutes in a 350° oven.

serve with: Cold shrimps with a melted-butter dip seasoned with prepared mustard with drinks, white rice, mixed green salad with mandarin orange sections, and a frozen chocolate chiffon pie for dessert.
The wine should be a light red, such as California Zinfandel.

QUICK-PREPARATION DINNERS

SAVORY LAMB STEAKS

Serves 2

2 ounces blue cheese, preferably   2 dashes Tabasco
  Roquefort   2 lamb steaks, ¾ to 1
1 small clove garlic, crushed   inch thick

1. Mash the cheese to a paste, blending in the garlic and Tabasco.
2. Spread each side of steak with paste, using half of it.
3. Broil five minutes, 3 inches from the broiler flame.
4. Turn steaks over and spread with the rest of the paste. Broil three or four minutes more, until steaks are cooked through.

serve with: Raw vegetable bites with a sour-cream dip with drinks, packaged herb-flavored rice, broccoli, French rolls, and sweet butter. Frozen pecan pie for dessert.
The wine should be a robust red, a Chianti or a Burgundy.

CALIFORNIA HAM STEAK

Serves 4

2 center-cut ham slices, about   2 tart cooking apples
  ¾ inches thick   Cloves
  Prepared mustard   Cinnamon
  Brown sugar   Calvados or brandy

1. Preheat oven to 400°.

2. Lay one slice of the ham on an oven-to-table baking dish. Spread lightly with mustard and put about a ⅛-inch layer of brown sugar over that.

3. Peel and core the apples and slice into neat ¼-inch rings. Lay them on the ham slice, covering as much of the ham as possible.

4. Cover with second slice and repeat mustard and brown sugar and apples. Stud between the apples with whole cloves. Dust very lightly with cinnamon.

5. Bake for twenty-five to thirty minutes. Place Calvados or brandy in a ladle or large tablespoon and warm over a low flame, then pour over ham and set alight. Rush to table before the flames die down.

serve with: Almond Cheese Balls (page 64) with drinks, packaged herb-flavored rice, frozen baby lima beans, and chocolate-chip-mint ice cream for dessert.

The wine should be a Chablis or a chilled rosé.

KIDNEYS À LA FRANÇAISE

Serves 2

2 tablespoons butter, at room temperature	Pinch mace
	Salt
½ teaspoon minced parsley	Pepper
½ teaspoon chervil	1 scallion, white part only, minced
½ teaspoon tarragon	2 veal or 6 lamb kidneys (you may
½ teaspoon chives	have to ask the butcher in
Pinch thyme	advance)
Pinch mustard	

1. Cream butter with minced herbs, seasonings, and scallions. Leave at room temperature.

2. Remove tissuelike outer skin from kidneys. Cut in half. Remove cores with curved nail scissors.

3. Melt butter and seasonings over very low heat, add kidneys, and toss gently to coat. Remove from butter and remove butter to cool.

4. Place kidneys, cut side down, on broiler rack and broil, 4 inches from

heat, for five minutes. Turn and broil three more minutes. Divide herbed butter equally into kidney "cups" and serve at once on very hot plates.

serve with: Baked Stuffed Clams (page 72) with drinks, instant mashed potatoes mixed with egg yolk and grated cheese, mixed green salad, and frozen or bakery napoleons for dessert.

The wine should be a very light red, such as a Cabernet Sauvignon.

CREOLE PORK CHOPS

Serves 2

4 thick pork chops	¼ teaspoon thyme
2 tomatoes, sliced	¼ teaspoon sage
1 large onion, sliced	1 cup chicken broth
1 green pepper, chopped	½ cup dry white wine
Salt	⅔ cup raw rice
Pepper	

1. Preheat oven to 350°.

2. Use the fat edge of one chop to grease a heavy iron skillet, then brown chops on both sides and place in a casserole.

3. Arrange tomatoes, onion, and green pepper on chops and season with salt, pepper, thyme, and sage.

4. Heat broth and wine together in a saucepan. Sprinkle raw rice into casserole around chops, and pour hot broth-and-wine mixture over.

5. Cover casserole and bake for forty-five minutes, or until all liquid is gone and rice is tender.

serve with: Anchovy Toast Fingers (page 70) with drinks, mixed green salad with Classic French Dressing (page 76) and Roquefort cheese crumbled over, salted bread sticks, and frozen cheesecake for dessert.

The wine should be a red Bordeaux or another light, dry red.

BEEF MARILI

Serves 2

1 slice bread
¾ pound ground round or chuck
1 egg
¼ teaspoon salt
⅛ teaspoon pepper
⅛ teaspoon nutmeg

2 tablespoons grated Parmesan
  cheese
Flour
1 beaten egg
  Dry bread crumbs
2 tablespoons butter

1. Soak the bread in water, then squeeze it dry.
2. Mix bread with the meat, egg, seasonings and cheese.
3. Form the mixture into two ovals about ½ inch thick.
4. Dip into flour, then beaten egg, then into bread crumbs.
5. Melt butter in frying pan, and fry meat over medium flame until brown, about five minutes on each side.

serve with: Oysters or clams on the half-shell with drinks, heated canned tomato sauce with mushrooms for the meat in a separate sauce boat, frozen baked potatoes heated in the oven and sprinkled with chopped parsley, frozen green peas with baby onions, Harvey's Chocolate Pots (page 86) for dessert.

The wine should be a robust red, such as a Pinot Noir.

ROAST BEEF FOR TWO

Serves 2

  Salt
Pepper
1 rib of a standing rib roast, about
  2½ pounds

2 large baking potatoes

1. One or two days before, ask your butcher to cut the meat for you and tie it round with string so that it will stand up. Then have him freeze it *solid.*
2. On cooking day, one hour and fifteen minutes before dinner, preheat

the oven to 400°. Salt and pepper the frozen meat on both sides and place scrubbed potatoes on each side to hold it upright, in a standing position.

3. Roast in a baking pan, for one hour and fifteen minutes for rare inside (add ten minutes for medium rare). Let stand about five minutes before carving, into two slices. The insides of each piece will be rare, the outsides browned and well done.

serve with: Smoked salmon on rye-pumpernickel rounds sprinkled with coarse ground black pepper with drinks, hot rolls, mixed green salad with Classic French Dressing (page 76) and Roquefort crumbled over, buttered asparagus and coffee ice cream topped with Kahlúa for dessert.

The wine should be a Burgundy or a Pinot Noir.

ROCK LOBSTER TAILS

Serves 2

Two 5-ounce or 6-ounce
  boxes frozen lobster
  tails, thawed
Small metal skewers

¼ pound butter
4 drops Tabasco
1 small clove garlic, crushed

1. With a sharp knife, cut through the hard top of the lobster tail, cutting the shell but not the thin underside. Spread open, butterfly style, so meat is exposed. Run small metal skewer sideways through lobster, so that it will stay flat under heat.

2. Melt butter, add Tabasco and garlic, and pour about 1 tablespoon over each lobster tail.

3. Broil, 4 to 5 inches from heat, for eight or nine minutes. Baste with butter sauce twice during broiling, and serve with leftover butter sauce in two bowls, for dunking individual bites.

serve with: Baked Stuffed Mushrooms (page 70) with drinks, frozen potato puffs, cold asparagus with Vinaigrette Dressing (page 79), and angelfood cake with frozen raspberries and whipped cream for dessert.

The wine should be a chilled Riesling.

5 Easy Ways to Begin a Dinner

Recipes for when you're in a hurry
and some for when you plan ahead.

MAKE-AHEAD APPETIZERS

BRANDIED PÂTÉ

¼ cup butter
2 small cans mushrooms
(bits and pieces, or
chop if whole)

2 cans Sell's Liver Pâté
¼ cup brandy, the best you can
afford

1. Melt butter over medium heat and sauté thoroughly drained mushrooms until well browned.

2. Add liver pâté, stirring well, then stir in brandy, off the fire.

3. Place in serving dish and refrigerate until needed. Serve with small round cocktail slices of rye bread.

HOT STUFFED CHEESE BALLS

A 5-ounce jar Kraft Old
English cheese
2 tablespoons butter
¾ cup sifted flour

Dash imported paprika
Dash Tabasco
A 4½-ounce can deviled ham

1. Preheat oven to 350°.

2. With a wooden spoon, blend together cheese and butter; then add flour, paprika, and Tabasco and knead to a smooth dough.

3. Make small balls of dough, about ¾ inch in diameter, and hollow out each ball in the palm of your hand with the thumb of your other hand. Fill hollows with deviled ham and pinch dough back together to completely encase ham.

4. Bake for ten to fifteen minutes and serve hot.

ALMOND CHEESE BALLS

6 ounces cream cheese
  A 5-ounce jar smokey cheese
  A 5-ounce jar blue cheese
  A 5-ounce jar cheese with bacon
½ teaspoon grated onion

¼ teaspoon Worcestershire sauce
¼ cup evaporated milk
  Dash angostura bitters
½ cup grated almonds

1. Have all ingredients at room temperature. In a large bowl, mix all ingredients but almonds together until well blended.

2. Pinch off small bits to make marble-sized balls and roll them in the grated almonds. Serve with Wheat Thins.

note: Make only as many balls as you think you'll need and keep the rest of the mixture, covered, under refrigeration. It keeps well.

CHEESE STICKS

1 cup flour
½ pound sharp Cheddar cheese, grated
½ cup butter or margarine, at room temperature

1 teaspoon cayenne
  Grated Romano cheese

1. Mix all ingredients except Romano and knead into a smooth flat ball. Wrap in waxed paper and chill for easier handling.

2. When dough is chilled, preheat oven to 450°. Lay a large sheet of waxed paper on a smooth surface and sprinkle lightly with grated Romano. Unwrap chilled dough and place on waxed paper. Sprinkle again with Romano and cover with another sheet of waxed paper. Roll into a rectangle about ⅛ inch thick and remove waxed paper. Cut into finger-sized strips with the aid of a sharp knife and a ruler.

4. Bake about four or five minutes, until crisp. Do not overbake: just barely cook them through.

DEVILED NUTS

½ cup salad oil
1 pound assorted nuts, shelled
½ teaspoon salt
1 tablespoon celery salt

¼ teaspoon cayenne
¼ teaspoon imported paprika
¼ teaspoon garlic salt

1. Preheat oven to 350°.

2. Pour the oil in a flat baking dish with sides and add the nuts, stirring to coat well.

3. Bake until nuts are toasted and golden, then lift onto paper towels to drain off excess oil. Place in bowl.

4. Mix seasonings together and add to nuts, stirring to coat well while still warm.

note: You can vary the seasonings, adding or subtracting as you like, but they should definitely have the cayenne and celery salt.

MUSHROOMS STUFFED WITH CAMEMBERT AND ALMONDS

10 to 12 medium raw mushrooms
 2 ounces Camembert or
   Liederkranz
¼ cup butter
 2 tablespoons minced parsley

2 tablespoons minced chives
  Dash Tabasco
  A 2-ounce package slivered
  almonds
2 tablespoons dry sherry

1. Wipe mushrooms and remove stems, saving them and leaving the caps intact. Place caps in a baking dish, hollow side up.

2. Cream together the cheese, butter, parsley, and chives.

3. Crush the almonds right in the package, using a rolling pin. Add almonds and Tabasco to cheese mixture. Stir in sherry.

4. Fill mushroom caps with the mixture and broil 3 inches from flame until hot and bubbly. They can be served cold, but are much better hot.

PICKLED VEGETABLES

12 small whole white boiling onions,
   peeled
 1 small cauliflower, broken into
   flowerets
½ pound small mushrooms
 2 green peppers, cut in 1-inch
   squares
18 black pitted olives

 1 cup olive oil
1½ cups white wine vinegar
 2 teaspoons salt
 ⅓ teaspoon freshly ground
   black pepper
 4 tablespoons sugar
 1 clove garlic, minced

1. Mix all the vegetables together in a large bowl.

2. Bring other ingredients to a boil and simmer gently for a few minutes. Let cool and pour over vegetables.

3. Cover and marinate twenty-four hours in the refrigerator.

4. Drain, reserving the marinade, and serve with toothpicks. If there's any left, cover with reserved marinade and refrigerate until needed again. They keep well.

BRANDIED ROQUEFORT SPREAD

An 8-ounce package cream
   cheese
1 pound Roquefort or blue cheese

3 tablespoons butter
¼ cup brandy, preferably cognac

1. Mash the cheese, add the butter, and mix all well together. If the cheeses are at room temperature, you can use the low speed of an electric mixer. Gradually add the brandy, blending well.

2. Refrigerate (or leave in the freezer for ten minutes) before serving. Serve with Melba Toast.

note: This makes a lot, but it improves with age.

RUMAKI

Makes 24

12 chicken livers
  Soy sauce
 8 water chestnuts

6 or 7 scallions
12 bacon slices, cut in half

1. Preheat oven to 450°.
2. Wash chicken livers, drain, and cut each in half. Cover with soy sauce.
3. Slice drained water chestnuts into three slices each.
4. Slit scallions lengthwise and cut into 1½-inch sections.
5. On a piece of chicken liver, lay a slice of water chestnut and a section of scallion. Wrap with half a slice of bacon and fasten with a toothpick. Lay the little bundles on a baking sheet and bake until bacon is crisp, about ten minutes.

note: These can be half-cooked, cooled, and then frozen or refrigerated for later use.

PICKLED SHRIMP

Serves 4

24 medium-to-large raw shrimp, in
   the shell
 1 stalk celery, chopped
 3 tablespoons pickling spice
1½ tablespoons salt
 ¾ cup salad oil

¼ cup white vinegar
¾ teaspoon salt
1¼ teaspoons celery seed
 1 tablespoon capers
  Dash Tabasco
 2 large mild onions

1. Cook shrimp in 1½ quarts boiling water with celery, pickling spice, and 1½ tablespoons salt for five minutes. Drain.
2. Combine oil, vinegar, ¾ teaspoon salt, celery seed, capers, and Tabasco.
3. Shell shrimp and slice onions into thin rings. In a large bowl, place a layer of onion, then a layer of shrimp, and repeat until all are used. Pour oil-vinegar mixture over, stir, and let stand in refrigerator for twenty-four hours.

SHRIMPS WITH ANCHOVY BUTTER

Serves 4 to 6

2 *pounds medium shrimp, raw and*
  shelled
2 *cans beer, opened and allowed to*
  stand until flat

½ *cup mixed pickling spice*
¾ *cup butter*
1 *teaspoon anchovy paste*

1. Slit the shelled shrimp down the vein side to "butterfly" them, but do not cut all the way through.

2. Put the flat beer in a large saucepan with the pickling spice and bring to a boil. Add shrimp and cook until just pink, about five minutes.

3. Place pan in refrigerator for one hour, then drain shrimp and return to refrigerator to chill completely. Cover.

4. At serving time, melt butter and stir in anchovy paste. Keep warm over a candle warmer and serve shrimp with toothpicks so they can be dipped into the warm butter.

SHRIMP PÂTÉ

½ *pound cooked, peeled, and*
  deveined shrimp, diced small
3 *tablespoons lemon juice*
½ *cup olive oil*

Salt
Freshly ground pepper
Paprika

Put the shrimp and lemon juice in a blender with ¼ cup of the olive oil. Blend well, adding the rest of the oil gradually to make a smooth paste. Season to taste with salt, pepper, and a generous dash of paprika. Serve with crackers, as a spread.

QUICK-PREPARATION APPETIZERS

ROQUEFORT CHEESE BALLS

4 ounces Roquefort cheese
½ cup butter
½ teaspoon dry mustard

4 tablespoons minced chives
2 tablespoons minced parsley

1. Mash together the cheese and butter with the mustard and form into marble-sized balls.

2. Mix together the chives and parsley and roll the balls in this to coat all over. Serve with toothpicks.

note: This mixture is delicious stuffed into cleaned raw mushroom caps and sprinkled with more chives. This amount will fill about twelve medium-sized mushrooms.

SALAMI–CREAM-CHEESE BITES

A 3-ounce package cream cheese
Heavy cream

5 slices large, mild salami

1. Break up the cream cheese in a bowl and add a little cream. Beat to a spreading consistency.

2. Lay a slice of salami on a flat surface and spread it with cream cheese, as smoothly as possible. Add another slice of salami, cover with waxed paper, and press as flat as possible with a plate. Remove waxed paper. Spread second slice of salami with cheese and repeat above process, then add another slice of salami, spread, and continue until all salami and cheese are used up.

3. Cut into squares with a sharp knife, spear each square with a toothpick, and serve.

ANCHOVY TOAST FINGERS

Makes 12

1 can anchovy fillets, undrained
2 teaspoons minced onion
2 tablespoons minced parsley
1 small clove garlic, minced
2 teaspoons olive oil

1 teaspoon lemon juice
3 slices firm white bread,
  cut into fingers, crusts
  removed

1. Preheat oven to 475°.
2. Place all ingredients except the bread in a blender and whir until well mixed, or mash anchovies with a fork and add the other ingredients.
3. Toast bread fingers under the broiler, quickly, on one side.
4. Spread untoasted side and bake five minutes. Serve at once.

MUSHROOM-PARSLEY ROLLS

16 to 18 thin slices firm bread
A 10½-ounce can condensed
  cream-of-mushroom soup

¼ cup minced parsley

1. Preheat oven to 450°.
2. Trim crusts from bread and discard. Spread each slice of bread with undiluted soup and sprinkle with parsley. Roll each slice up, starting at a corner, and fasten with a toothpick.
3. Bake for twelve to fifteen minutes, until golden. Serve hot.

BAKED STUFFED MUSHROOMS

Serves 4 to 6

24 large mushrooms
   Lemon juice
 3 tablespoons butter
¼ cup minced parsley
   Salt

   Pepper
¼ cup grated Parmesan cheese
 2 tablespoons minced onion
¼ cup sherry
½ cup fine dry bread crumbs

1. Preheat oven to 350°.

2. Wipe mushrooms with a damp cloth and remove stems, leaving caps intact. Mince stems fine. Sprinkle a few drops lemon juice into each cap and set aside.

3. Sauté minced stems in butter, then mix in parsley, salt, pepper, cheese, and onion. Stir in sherry to moisten, then add half the bread crumbs.

4. Pile into mushroom caps, sprinkle with more bread crumbs, and add a few dots butter on each cap.

5. Bake fifteen minutes and serve hot.

CREAM-CHEESE CUBES WITH SOY SAUCE AND SESAME SEEDS

½ cup sesame seeds   ½ cup soy sauce
A 3-ounce package cream
cheese

1. Toast the sesame seeds in a 350° oven for fifteen or twenty minutes, shaking the pan frequently.

2. Cut the cream cheese into twelve small cubes. Spear each with a toothpick.

3. Serve with a bowl of soy sauce and a bowl of sesame seeds. Dip a cube of cream cheese into the soy sauce, then into the sesame seeds, and eat.

TOASTED PARMESAN BREAD CUBES

Serves 4 to 6

Day-old French or Italian bread,   Sesame seeds
cut in twenty-four 1-inch cubes   Poppy seeds
1 cup butter, melted   Cayenne
1 cup grated Parmesan cheese

1. Preheat oven to 450°.

2. Quickly dip bread cubes in melted butter, then roll in grated Parmesan.

3. Lay on baking sheet. Sprinkle some with sesame seeds, some with poppy seeds, and some (lightly) with cayenne.

4. Bake five to ten minutes.

HOT HAM SNACKS

A 4½-ounce can deviled ham

2 tablespoons sour cream

1 tablespoon onion

2 teaspoons chopped freeze-dried
  chives

1 egg, lightly beaten

12 thin slices firm white bread

1. Preheat oven to 400°.

2. Combine all ingredients except bread and mix well.

3. Cut bread slices into circles about 2½ inches in diameter. Spread about 1 tablespoon of mixture onto each bread round.

4. Bake on cookie sheet for ten to twelve minutes and serve hot.

BAKED STUFFED CLAMS

⅓ cup fine dry bread crumbs

1 teaspoon chopped onion

1 teaspoon chopped green pepper

1 teaspoon chopped pimento

Dash Tabasco

Dash angostura bitters

1 dozen clams on the half-shell
  (these come canned)

2 tablespoons butter

1. Preheat oven to 350°.

2. Mix all ingredients except clams and butter.

3. Place one spoonful of mixture over each clam; dot with butter.

4. Bake ten minutes, until heated through.

6 Salads Made Simple

The rules are few, the results can be spectacular.

A salad can be a beautiful thing to look at and a joy forever to the digestion, or it can be a horrid hunk of quartered iceberg lettuce tasting only of the knife that cut it and smeared with a thick, ugly bright orange bottled dressing. Iceberg lettuce has no flavor that I can discern, and aside from its durability and its crisp texture, it is totally without character. And in a sandwich, it does go limp. Romaine stays beautifully crisp and tastes good.

Salad rules are few and simple. A mixed green, or tossed, salad should be just that: two or three different kinds of lettuce and greens, well washed and crisped either in your refrigerator crisper or in a brown paper bag or plastic container in the refrigerator. The crisp leaves are then torn by hand into bite-sized pieces and tossed with a dressing. I prefer to toss my salad with my hands, because I think metal imparts a taste. That's why wooden or china implements should be used to serve it, and why lettuce should never be cut with a knife.

The fresher the ingredients, the better. The most delicious salad I ever ate was in a French country inn, and a little baby white worm was wandering around in the lettuce. It had been washed, but not quite enough, after having been picked from the garden only minutes before. Of course, the salad was whisked away and another brought, and it was a memorable salad in the fresh goodness of its flavor. I have re-created it many times from my own gardens of lettuces and fresh herbs. The latter, by the way, do incredible things for salads (see Chapter 9, "The Basic Herbs and Spices").

There is a long list of lettuces you can usually find in your markets. Curly endive, long crisp romaine, delicate little Boston (sometimes called "butter") and Bibb, chicory, leaf lettuce, red leaf, and bronze. In some foreign markets, you can find lamb's quarters (or field salad), escarole, dandelion greens. Watercress and parsley, of course, are always around and always delicious. Occasionally you see Belgian or French endive, tightly furled small oblong heads that range in color from white to pale green. I think fresh Beluga caviar *may* be cheaper.

Nasturtium leaves are an interesting addition to a green salad, and so are celery leaves or celery seed. Garlic, to a true salad lover, is indispensable. You can rub your salad bowl with a cut clove of it, you can put it through a press into your dressing, or you can use what the French call a *chapon,* a piece of dry hard French bread rubbed with a cut clove of garlic and put into the salad for a faint and delicate aroma.

The pungent and aromatic leaves called "herbs" can add great variety and interest: chives, basil, tarragon, marjoram, oregano, and dill. Used in combination or singly, each contributes a newness to a plain tossed salad. You can add chopped fresh vegetables, too—celery, green onions, cucumbers, green peppers, carrots—but I much prefer the lettuces and herbs alone and the vegetables served in another way.

A plea for the tomato: they should be skinned. Hold speared on a fork, turning over a gas flame, until the skin bursts and peels right off. Or plunge tomatoes into boiling water for 60 seconds, then peel. Cut into quarters and scoop the seeds out. Then add at the last moment, so their juice does not dilute the dressing.

The classic French dressing for a salad is simple, too. Four parts of good olive oil to one part of wine vinegar or lemon juice, a pinch of salt, a grinding of pepper, and stir madly. It is obvious that there are infinite changes to be rung on this theme. The kind of vinegar you use will change its flavor. A pinch of dry mustard adds a little zip. How about a drop of Tabasco, or one of Worcestershire sauce? Use only three parts of oil to one of vinegar, and you have a more tart dressing. You simply have to stick a finger in and taste to get the exact flavor you want in your dressing.

So don't just toss the same mixed green salad every night. A salad is one of the most creative things you can make in a kitchen.

CLASSIC FRENCH DRESSING

4 tablespoons olive oil   Salt
1 tablespoon wine vinegar or lemon   Pepper
  juice

Mix all ingredients well, taste for seasoning, and pour over greens.

TART FRENCH DRESSING

3 tablespoons olive oil   Salt
1 tablespoon wine vinegar or lemon   Pepper
  juice

Follow the mixing directions for Classic French Dressing.

With these two dressings in your repertoire, you can then go on to embellish, with dry mustard, garlic, Tabasco, etc. I consider garlic and a pinch of mustard essential even to these simple dressings. But it is a matter of taste.

There are many good bottled dressings on the market, and when there isn't time to make your own, by all means use them. Most of the very good ones have their own special trade names and are not bottled by giant food corporations. Good mayonnaise is also more or less essential but can be deliciously doctored, as witness:

AVOCADO AND GRAPEFRUIT SALAD

1 avocado, peeled and sliced
  lengthwise

1 small can grapefruit segments
  Mayonnaise

Arrange these on lettuce (Boston or Bibb) on plates and pour over them a mayonnaise thinned with some of the grapefruit juice. The avocado should be peeled and sliced shortly before serving.

RICE SALAD

Serves 4

2 medium carrots, chopped fine
2 celery stalks, chopped fine
2 small scallions, chopped fine
½ green pepper, chopped fine
8 green olives, chopped
8 black olives, chopped
1 cup minced fresh parsley
½ teaspoon dried tarragon leaves
4 anchovy fillets, rinsed and
  chopped

1½ cups white rice, cooked and
    cooled (measured before
    cooking)
1 cup mayonnaise
  Olive oil
  Oil from the anchovy can
  (optional)
  Salt
  Freshly ground black pepper

1. Mix all the vegetables. Crush the tarragon leaves between your palms and add them and the anchovy bits. Combine with the rice, mixing well.

2. Thin the mayonnaise with olive oil until it is like heavy cream, using

a few drops of the anchovy oil from the can, if you like anchovies very much. Taste and check for saltiness (anchovies are very salty).

3. Stir this sauce into the rice mixture, grind pepper over it, and chill well.

note: The traditional Italian salad served with Vitello Tonnato uses one cup of the veal-tuna sauce served over the veal. But the salad is so good, and so unexpected a pleasant surprise, that I worked out this version using a thinned mayonnaise and extra anchovies. You won't need them if you serve it with Vitello Tonnato (page 24).

A friend in San Francisco, finding himself with guests and without vinegar or lemon juice for a salad, substituted gin, to everybody's great delight. You can't taste what makes the difference. It's just differently delicious. Subsequent attempts using dry vermouth were equally successful.

This is best on a mixture of Boston lettuce and romaine, with a finely minced green onion added to the greens.

GIN SALAD

4 tablespoons olive oil
2 tablespoons gin
  Dash Tabasco
1 clove garlic, mashed

Pinch dry mustard
Salt and coarsely ground black
pepper to taste

Mix all ingredients thoroughly and let sit, stirring occasionally, until serving time. Then pour over greens, toss, and serve.

note: A little more gin can be added, but not so much that you identify its flavor as such.

ARTICHOKES WITH VINAIGRETTE DRESSING

Artichokes are so very good that I wish they didn't intimidate so many people. They're very easy. With a sharp knife, cut off about an inch and a half of the tops, and cut off the stems. Drop into a pot of boiling water to which you've added about a tablespoon of olive oil, a good dash of vinegar, and a garlic clove. Cook, covered, about twenty-five minutes, or until an outside leaf pulls off easily. Use tongs for this. Set some of the cooking liquid aside. Then lift out and drain them, upside down in a colander. When cool enough to handle, place an artichoke in a cup and gently separate the leaves. In the center, start digging down with a sharp spoon and pulling out the fuzzy "choke," leaving the artichoke bottom as intact as possible. Then cool completely and they're ready to be filled with Vinaigrette Dressing. (The recipe below is enough dressing for two artichokes.)

VINAIGRETTE DRESSING

3 tablespoons olive oil
1 tablespoon cider, wine, or
   tarragon vinegar
   Salt
   Pepper
1 teaspoon tarragon
1 teaspoon chervil

Imported paprika
1 finely chopped hard-cooked egg
1 teaspoon capers
1 teaspoon chopped parsley
1 teaspoon chives
1 tablespoon liquid in which you
   cooked the artichokes

Mix all well together and fill the artichoke centers, dribbling any extra dressing down between the leaves.

note: This is equally good on cold artichokes, asparagus, cauliflower, or green beans.

SPINACH SALAD

1 head of spinach	1 egg yolk
½ cup mayonnaise	Salt
1 tablespoon catsup	Pepper
1 tablespoon bottled Thousand	Lemon juice (optional)
Island dressing	Crisp bacon bits
1 tablespoon olive oil	1 hard-cooked egg, chopped

1. Separate the spinach leaves and remove the stems. Wash the leaves well. Crisp the spinach in ice water, dry on paper towels, and refrigerate in plastic bag.

2. Mix mayonnaise, catsup, Thousand Island dressing, and olive oil together, and beat in the raw egg yolk. Taste for salt and pepper, or perhaps a dash of lemon juice.

3. Toss spinach with dressing and pile onto salad plates. Garnish with bacon bits and finely chopped hard-cooked egg.

SPINACH AND WATERCRESS SALAD

Follow directions for Spinach Salad (above), adding a good handful (about half a bunch) of watercress leaves, stripped of the stems, mixed in with the spinach.

ZUCCHINI AND RAW MUSHROOM SALAD

Two zucchini, 3 to 4 inches long	4 mushrooms
2 tablespoons olive oil	1 head romaine
3 tablespoons salad oil	
1½ teaspoons vinegar	
1 tablespoon Durkee dressing (or dash Tabasco, dash Worcestershire, salt, and pepper)	

1. Wash the zucchini, cut off ends, cut into quarters. Sauté briefly in 1 tablespoon of the olive oil, turn heat low, cover, and let cook until just barely tender, about ten minutes.

2. While the zucchini is cooking, make a dressing of the remaining 1 tablespoon olive oil and the salad oil, vinegar, and seasoning.

3. Wash the mushrooms and slice. Put mushrooms and zucchini in a bowl, add dressing. Cover and marinate until serving time.

4. Wash and tear the lettuce. Dry and break into salad bowl. Pour dressing and vegetables over and toss before serving.

7 Easy Ways to End a Dinner

Cold or hot, quick or when-you-have-time recipes.

I don't really care for sweets, except on very rare occasions. To finish off my dinner, I like fruits and cheese, in all their myriad and wonderful combinations, which you can keep on hand to make a quick dessert, or a snack, or a breakfast.

Sweet drinks are a good dessert. When I was first introduced to Irish Coffee, I thought I could drink it forever. Black Russians are especially good at the end of a meal, although I can drink only one.

But there are a few quick things you can make ahead that are utterly delicious. The make-ahead desserts that follow are all light, delicate, and not too terribly rich in calories. They do not lie in the stomach like triplets, as do so many cloying, synthetically sweet desserts and pastries. The quick ones involve either fruit or liquor.

MAKE-AHEAD DESSERTS

CRÈME BRÛLÉE

Serves 4 to 6

4 eggs
4 tablespoons sugar
2 cups warm milk
1 teaspoon vanilla extract (real, not vanilla flavoring)

Butter
¾ cup brown sugar

1. Beat eggs until light with sugar, adding warm milk as you beat. Stir in vanilla and then set aside. Preheat oven to 325°.

2. Butter lavishly a 3-inch-deep Pyrex or ceramic baking dish. Then put the brown sugar in and place the dish over a *low* flame, swirling the dish around as the sugar begins to melt and caramelize. It will only take two to three minutes.

3. When the sugar is caramel brown, remove from flame and tilt so that the caramel covers the sides as well as the bottom. Pour in the custard.

4. Place dish in a baking pan containing one inch of hot water and bake slowly (so that the water barely simmers) about forty minutes, or until a silver knife inserted in the center comes out clean.

5. Remove from oven, place a serving dish over the top, and turn upside down, so the caramel will run down the sides of the cooked custard. Allow to cool, uncovered, then refrigerate until serving time. The caramel will harden, and you must crack it with your serving spoon, which is part of the fun if you serve it at the table.

CHOCOLATE-WAFER—WHIPPED-CREAM DESSERT

Serves 4

1 cup heavy cream
2 tablespoons sugar

24 chocolate wafers (part of an 8½ -
    ounce box)

1. Whip cream until thick; then add sugar gradually and continue whipping until sugar is absorbed and cream is stiff.

2. For each serving, layer 6 thin chocolate wafers with cream between on a serving plate, adding a final dollop of cream on the top.

3. Set in freezing compartment of refrigerator for one hour, then place in refrigerator overnight to "mellow."

note: After the hour in the freezer, you can swirl more whipped cream around the sides for further decoration, or sprinkle the tops with colored or chocolate sprinkles.

HARVEY'S LITTLE CHOCOLATE POTS OR CHOCOLATE CUSTARD

1 cup semisweet chocolate bits
2 egg yolks

3 tablespoons bourbon or brandy
1¼ cup light cream, scalded

1. Put the chocolate bits in the blender, add egg yolks, and add brandy or bourbon.

2. Scald the cream (which means heat it just until bubbles start to appear at the edge of the pot) and pour it into the blender.

3. Let the blender whir until the mixture is well blended. Pour it into six little pots or a suitable dish with high sides. Chill until firm.

CHOCOLATE RUM ROLL

Batter

Cooking oil
Waxed paper
5 eggs, separated

¾ cup flour
5 tablespoons sugar
Powdered sugar

Filling

1 square unsweetened
  chocolate
6 ounces semisweet chocolate
  bits
3 tablespoons cold water

3 tablespoons butter
1 tablespoon rum
½ cup chopped walnuts
Several large pieces of walnut to
garnish, if desired

1. Preheat oven to 350°.

2. Oil a baking sheet liberally with cooking oil, line with waxed paper, and oil the paper liberally too.

3. Beat the egg whites until stiff. Mix the flour and 5 tablespoons sugar into the yolks, beating lightly to blend. Fold the egg whites into the egg yolk mixture, gently. (The batter should look like pale yellow soapsuds.)

4. Spread batter evenly into the prepared baking sheet and bake fifteen minutes, until golden.

5. While batter cooks, sift powdered sugar over a clean dishcloth laid on a flat surface. When the batter is cooked, turn upside down onto the sugared dishcloth. With the aid of a sharp knife, peel off the waxed paper and, lifting the corners of the towel to help it get started, roll up the roll like a jelly roll. Put it in the refrigerator to cool.

5. Put chocolate, chocolate bits, and 3 tablespoons water in top of double boiler over hot water. Stir until chocolate melts and mixture is smooth. Add 3 tablespoons butter and stir in, remove from heat, and add rum and chopped nuts.

6. Stir over a bowl of ice until it starts to thicken. Remove roll from refigerator, unroll on waxed paper, and spread filling over it, reserving ½ cup. Roll up again and decorate with reserved filling. Space pieces of walnut along for decoration if desired. Lift, with the aid of the waxed paper, to serving platter. Cut away excess waxed paper and cool until serving time.

RHEA'S FRUIT DESSERT

1 10-oz. package frozen mixed fruit

1 10-oz. package frozen raspberries

1 sliced banana, 1 small can
    pineapple chunks, or
    coconut flakes (optional)

2 tablespoons granulated sugar

1 cup sour cream

3 tablespoons dark brown sugar

4 tablespoons gin or bourbon

1. Thaw fruits and drain juices into a pan, add granulated sugar, and cook until the juices form a thick syrup.

2. Add this syrup, after cooling, to drained fruits and stir well.

3. Stir in all other ingredients and chill thoroughly.

COLD LEMON MOLD

Serves 4 to 6

1 tablespoon gelatin

4 tablespoons cold water

2 eggs

1 cup granulated sugar

3 tablespoons fresh lemon juice

1 tablespoon grated lemon rind

1 cup heavy cream, whipped

1. Soak the gelatin for a few minutes in cold water in the top of a double boiler, then place over hot water and stir until dissolved.

2. Beat eggs, adding sugar gradually, until light and fluffy, then beat in dissolved gelatin, lemon juice, and lemon rind.

3. Fold in the whipped cream and pour into a mold rinsed in cold water.

4. Refrigerate for at least four hours before unmolding to serve.

note: To unmold, dip mold in warm water for just a second, then place serving plate upside down over mold and turn over. The molded dessert should drop right onto the plate. Refrigerate again until served.

Traditionally, the French dessert that follows is made in a special heart-shaped wicker basket. However, you can make it using a large sieve instead of the basket. Or use a colander—anything that will allow it to drain overnight.

COEUR À LA CRÈME (STRAWBERRY CREAM-CHEESE HEART)

½ *pound cream cheese*
½ *pound cottage cheese, drained*
  Dash salt

1 *cup heavy cream*
1 *box fresh whole strawberries,*
  washed and hulled

1. Beat together the cream cheese, cottage cheese, and salt until very smooth. (A hand mixer is ideal, or use a rotary beater.)
2. Gradually add the cream and continue beating until smooth again.
3. Line your basket, sieve or whatever with wet cheesecloth, place over a deep bowl, and pour in the cheese mixture. Refrigerate overnight so that it can drain.

to serve: Turn out onto a suitable dish, surround with fresh strawberries and take to table.

ZABAGLIONE

Serves 4 to 6

6 *egg yolks*
6 *teaspoons sugar*

6 *tablespoons Marsala*

1. Combine these ingredients in the top of a double boiler over hot, but not boiling, water. Start beating them with a rotary egg beater.
2. From time to time, scrape down the sides of the pan, removing it from the heat, then returning it and continuing to beat until the mixture is thick and fluffy and rises in the pan. This will take about eight minutes.
3. Remove from heat at once and continue to beat until slightly cooled, then pour into sherbet glasses and refrigerate until serving time.

QUICK-PREPARATION DESSERTS

BLACK RUSSIANS

Makes 1 drink

2 *ounces vodka*   *Heavy cream (optional)*
¾ *ounce Kahlúa*

Stir vodka and Kahlúa together in a short glass of cracked ice, and float about a teaspoon of cream over the top, if desired.

PEACHES IN CHAMPAGNE

1 peach per serving   Brut *champagne, as needed*

1. Peel peaches by plunging, individually, into boiling water for one minute, then slipping skins off.
2. Prick all over with a fork, then place in champagne glass and fill with champagne.
3. Serve with dinner, the champagne to be sipped and replenished as needed, then the peach eaten for dessert.

PEARS POACHED IN RED WINE

Serves 4

4 *fresh pears*   *A small strip of lemon peel*
2 *cups dry red wine*   ½ *cup port*
½ *cup sugar*
   A few drops red food coloring

1. Peel pears carefully, leaving stems on.
2. Make a syrup by boiling together the red wine and sugar, with the lemon peel twisted in and the food coloring added drop by drop until the syrup is a good red color.

3. Slide the pears into the syrup and let them simmer gently ten to fifteen minutes, until a toothpick inserted near the bottom finds them still firm but cooked.

4. Remove pears with a wooden spoon, or two wooden spoons, carefully so you don't mark them, and set them in a deep serving dish.

5. Add the port to the syrup and simmer gently a few more minutes; then pour hot syrup over pears and let cool. Refrigerate covered overnight, if wished. Serve cold.

IRISH COFFEE

Serves 4

4 *large, short-stemmed glasses*	3 *cups hot black coffee*
Hot water	4 *jiggers Irish whisky (6 ounces)*
12 *small lumps sugar (6 teaspoons)*	4 *tablespoons whipped cream*

1. Put the glasses on a tray and fill them with hot (not boiling) water. Then pour the water out and put 3 lumps, or 1½ teaspoons, sugar in each glass.

2. Fill the glasses about half full of hot, strong coffee and add a jigger (1½ ounces) Irish whisky. Stir quickly to melt the sugar.

3. Carefully float 1 tablespoon whipped heavy cream (*real* whipped cream) on top of each glass and serve.

serious warning: People will think they can drink this delicious concoction forever. Do not let them. Seconds, in clean glasses, are permissible, but after three, when they stand up their knees will bend backward.

8 The Really Basic Equipment

A discussion of pots, pans, and tools, and some sensible advice on the selection of dishes and flatware.

Basic cooking equipment depends on how you cook, and what. However, certain pots, pans and utensils are essential to modern cooking. People can eat with the aid of nothing more than a knife and some fingers. And if you've got a fire you can poke a stick into something edible and cook it. You may even have a shaggy dog around to wipe fingers on, as any medieval painting will show you. Remember, forks were considered a foppish Italian invention when first introduced at the French court. But we are talking now about what I like to think of as civilized cooking.

So the really basic pieces you need are a frying pan, or skillet, and two pots, one slightly larger than the other. With these, you can "make do." Let's discuss frying pans first. Since I must of necessity do a lot of cooking for experimentation, I have three kinds, in a variety of sizes. But if I could only have *one,* it would be of black cast iron, of a good size, with a lid. In this, I can pan-broil a steak or chop when it is heated hot-hot and sprinkled with salt, or in one corner of it I can gently sauté or scramble an egg. With the lid on, I've got a braising pan for stews or pot roast or Swiss steak or other dishes of that kind. In other words, a casserole.

My second choice of frying pan would be Le Creuset ware, enamel over cast iron, obtainable from Bazar Français, 666 Sixth Avenue, New York, N.Y. 10022. If you write, they will send you a catalogue. One of these pans I reserve exclusively for omelets, and the others I use for chicken pieces, scaloppine and foods like that. This ware is heavy, but remarkably easy to clean (after cooling, fill it with warm water and allow to soak for a few minutes). There are American and imported versions which are much cheaper, but Le Creuset is the best.

My third kind of frying pan is admittedly an extravagance. It is tin-lined copper from Bazar Français. It must be handled with great care, since the tin lining will melt at high temperatures. Its great virtue is that it doesn't *need* high temperature. The copper conducts heat quickly and evenly over a low flame. If you use electric heat, and fuel consumption is of interest to you, it is worth the investment. Besides, it is very decorative to hang in your kitchen.

You do have other choices. Tin (which is too thin), light-weight aluminum, which always sticks for me, and electric, for which I would not give you a plugged Mexican peso. However, I do know people who cook, and very well indeed, with both these last two named and would make them their first choice. Mine is still black iron, if I can only have one kind. Yes,

I know there is a supposedly nonstick lined kind of cookware, and I will give you my expurgated opinion of that right now. I loathe it. Foods *do* stick, you must use special tools to lift things from it, and it scratches at the slightest touch of metal, thereby enabling things to stick more.

Now we come to pots. Or saucepans. You must have two, one slightly larger than the other. The little one can be used over the other as a kind of double boiler, in an emergency. My personal preference is enamel over steel, white inside and colored outside. I have two pots, a frying pan, a double boiler, a coffeepot into which I pour my own "saucepan" coffee (see page 98), and a casserole. They are extremely easy to keep clean. A little scouring powder on a sponge does both insides and outsides, and with the white insides you can *see* that they are clean. I also cherish a La Creuset saucepan, heavy but perfect for cooking vegetables in practically no water.

And I have cooked, with success, in pots of very heavy aluminum. My friend Esther Campbell and I have done everything from a stuffed goose to a sixteen-inch cold poached salmon, decorated most elaborately like a picture in one of her French cookbooks. Her pots are of very heavy aluminum, smooth inside and dimpled outside, and a vast assortment of Mexican earthenware. They all work very well for me—the aluminum on top of the stove, the earthenware for oven dishes. Esther got her earthenware in Mexico; in this country you can buy a brand called "Redwing" that is remarkably durable. I have one casserole of it, and I would replace it at once if it got broken.

I also use my La Creuset casseroles constantly. I have three—a small two-person one, a good-sized oval one, and a huge one that, when full, I can't lift. But I can always get help in lifting it when it is full of something like paella or a cassoulet. These are all stove-to-table ware, as is the pottery and/or earthenware.

Equally invaluable to me are my two Dru-iron baking dishes. They are white inside, blue outside, enamel over iron, twelve and fourteen inches long with two-and-one-half-inch sides. They were presents, and you can find similar American-made ones. You should have one, at least.

The year that Esther and I fixed Mr. Salmon so beautifully, I spent hours making a mayonnaise for him in the traditional way, with a china platter and a silver fork. Last year, Esther had acquired a blender, and made mayonnaise in about four minutes flat. I have one of the original blenders, with one speed, and I have used it and loved it for more than twenty years. In it, I make my drinkable breakfast (I can't face food in the morning), and a superb Vichyssoise from frozen potato soup, hollandaise, mayonnaise (now), black bean soup and Harvey's Chocolate Pots (or Custard). For these alone, it is worth getting your hands on a blender. And you'll find many other uses for it, as well. Get one. Even if it is just the cheapest, it is a good investment. You don't *need* eight speeds, do you?

I also use my little tin-lined copper Bazar Français *au gratin* dishes a great deal, but china ones would do equally well. I use them for egg dishes, individual seafood Newburgs, and many other dishes when I wish each person to have an individual serving. These I consider essential to my kind of cooking, but you may not.

As a matter of fact, it is quite possible to make a delicious meal with *no* pots or pans. One year we bought a beach house in South Laguna. It was very cheap, totally adequate for our needs, and hideous beyond belief inside. All of the woodwork had been painted bright shiny red, green or blue enamel. The bedroom had three different wallpapers. The kitchen, which was dark to begin with, had black paper with a Chinese motif. Since I am what is called "handy" with my hands, and have had years of experience fixing up the insides of houses, which I adore doing, I went down the next weekend armed with lots of paint, paint remover, wallpaper remover and empty coffee cans, which I use for washing out paint brushes.

A good friend arrived later with large and beautiful lamb chops, and my stove wasn't hooked up as yet. We constructed an outdoor barbecue grill from bricks out of the yard, one of the oven racks laid over, and we made a delightful dinner of tiny red new potatoes boiled in one coffee can, fresh peas smothered with butter and cooked on a bed of lettuce with snippets of little green onions and a leaf of mint which Robert went and found, all in another coffee can, and the broiled chops. Water for our coffee heated in a third can while we ate. This brings me to the recipe for the coffee, which I learned as a girl out camping with my parents and have never found a better.

COFFEE

4 cups

4 cups water
4 heaping tablespoons regular-
    grind coffee and about ½
    tablespoon for the pot

Heat the water to boiling in a saucepan. Dump in the coffee and stir quickly for the count of three. Turn heat off and add ¼ cup cold water to settle the grounds. Let coffee sit for a few minutes to brew, then strain into a coffeepot through a fine strainer and serve. This is good strong coffee, with a wonderful flavor and aroma. And you can make it in *anything* that will hold water and can be put over a fire.

Another friend in San Francisco, a painter named Robert Harvey, introduced me to another kind of pot that is ideal for busy people who also like to entertain. Harvey has a chicken pot, of ceramic, made in the shape of a chicken. The secret of these pots is to choose your chicken so that it fits with no more than one-half inch of space around it in the pot, and to make sure the lid fits snugly. (You can truss up a slightly-too-large bird to fit the pot.) And then all you have to do is season the bird inside and out, cover with the top, put it in the oven, follow the manufacturer's directions that come with the pot for temperature and timing, and forget it until you are ready to serve. The chicken, miraculously, will be golden and crisp-skinned with no attention from you, and it will be fork-tender. These pots are certainly worth tracking down if time out of the kitchen is important to you.

If you want to do chic cooking, you will need a pie pan for Quiche Lorraine. The very prettiest is an ovenproof white china one with fluted sides, imported from France. It costs about twelve dollars, which is "ouch" in anybody's language, unless you are rich or given one, as I was. The next most attractive is Pyrex, which isn't too expensive, and then there are the ones you can buy in the supermarket. If that's what you can afford, buy it and serve your quiche onto individual plates in the kitchen before you bring it out. It is, after all, the *food* that is important, not the pan in which it was cooked.

If you are very dessert-conscious, you will need a couple of cake pans and a cookie sheet with half-inch sides. As for soufflés, I have made them in everything from an earthenware casserole to a Pyrex mixing bowl, and while they don't look as glamorous when brought to table as the ones in the classic white china soufflé dish, they taste just as good.

Now we come to essential tools. First of all, knives. I will *not* recommend anything but the best, which are French chef's knives. They're expensive, but you can start with a small one for mincing small things and a large one for heavier work. They have a triangular blade, balance nicely in your hand, and are not made of stainless steel, which will not take or hold an edge. The French ones take, and hold, a razor edge. And when you can afford a third, get the long thin slicing and boning knife. Many large cities have restaurant supply houses, and houses that buy equipment (slightly used) from going-out-of-business restaurants. Snoop into those if you can. You will find wonderful bargains.

Next, you need spoons to stir with. I prefer wooden ones, sold very cheaply in the supermarket. And a couple of rubber or plastic spatulas, a long thin narrow one and a wider, blunt-bottomed one. You will also need a slotted spoon, for lifting things out of hot water, and metal kitchen tongs. Add a pancake turner, a curved two-tined fork, a wire whisk, a little strainer and a larger one, an egg beater (all supermarket items), and you're in business.

I do not believe in going out and buying everything you see for the kitchen. The pleasant way, I have discovered through experience, is to acquire your basics and start cooking. People will soon start giving you kitchen equipment as presents. Nice big things, like copper or Dru-iron or casseroles—and even nice little things like a Mouli grater for cheese and a baby nutmeg grater for fresh nutmeg, which add incredible zest to all sorts of vegetables and other dishes.

I will *not* recommend any kind of plastic tableware, unless you have children who throw things on the floor and you haven't started teaching them table manners early. I do not recommend having "good" dishes that you bring out only for guests. If it is good enough for company, it is good enough for you to enjoy as well. When you are just starting out with dishes, I would recommend plain white place settings. Your food looks better and there is no design to confuse the eye. You can always add colored dishes and fun dishes later.

When it comes to your table flatware, you can buy very inexpensive stainless steel, moderately priced stainless steel, and very expensive stainless steel—all of them in a range of patterns so wide and varied you'd have to like one of them. I would rather have the good stainless than silver-plate, which is an imitation, because I hate imitation anythings. But if you can afford silver, buy *only the best.* It is heavy in the hand, and Tiffany, for example, has never discontinued a pattern. With companies of this repute, you can buy exactly the pieces you need, adding others as you go along. And you can always add serving pieces, and extra teaspoons, or replace any pieces that get lost.

ABSOLUTELY ESSENTIAL

1 knife

HELPFUL TO HAVE

1 heavy frying pan, with lid, to double as a casserole
2 saucepans, one slightly larger than the other
1 stove-to-table baking dish
1 pie pan
1 baking sheet with ½-inch sides
2 knives, 1 small and 1 large

wooden spoons
pancake turner
slotted spoon
metal tongs
2-tined curved fork
wire whisk
rubber or plastic spatula
1 strainer

9 The Basic Herbs and Spices

Their uses and their affinities for foods.

If I had a dollar for every time someone has asked me the difference between herbs and spices, I would be rich beyond measure. It is really very simple, but they are lumped together in what seems one word, "herbs-andspices," in the young cook's mind.

Herbs are the aromatic leaves of plants grown in temperate climates. Their virtues have been known since earliest recorded history, both as medicines and as a means of making food taste better.

Spices are the dried seeds, roots and bark of trees and bushes grown in the tropics. Their history is decidedly romantic. Marco Polo brought some of them back from his travels and thus inspired a long and very brisk political intrigue as to which of the European countries should own the "Spice Islands." Europe needed them to keep food from spoiling, to mask the tastes of somewhat spoiled foods, and in general to make their bland food edible. Wars were fought, raids were undertaken, ships plundered. The Dutch, Germans, French, Spanish and English ran ships around the world to garner these precious spices, and they used them as lavishly as they could afford. Some of the Elizabethan and earlier recipes stagger the imagination with their spicing and sweetening of meat.

The basic HERBS that you will use almost constantly are basil, bay leaves (or laurel), marjoram, oregano, tarragon and parsley. I recommend very strongly that you buy them all, except parsley, in whole leaf form and crush them slightly in the palm of your hand before adding them to a dish. Parsley can always be found fresh, and keeps indefinitely in a covered jar in the refrigerator. Snip the leaves off the stems with scissors before storing, then chop or snip into fine shreds to use.

Bay, parsley and thyme flavor almost every stew or soup. Basil has a notable affinity for tomatoes; basil, oregano and marjoram, together and separately, have one for veal; and tarragon has one for chicken.

Many books will tell you that you can grow herbs in a window box, or on a shelf in little pots. What they neglect to tell you is that herbs require full sunshine. I know. I had them growing feet high, in South Laguna, because by luck the place I planted them got full sunshine. When I moved back to Los Angeles and planted again, they got up about three inches, the trees came into leaf and shaded them, and they all died. But a salad made with *fresh* herbs, any or all, is like no other salad in the world. Even people who don't like salad say Wow! and ask for second helpings. I don't think you can taste that much difference if you use the dried leaves in cooked dishes, however, unless you have a very educated palate.

SPICES flavor quite another kettle. Pepper, of course, is a spice and we use it daily in almost everything. But cinnamon, cloves and nutmeg, spices all, are most commonly used in baking. Freshly grated nutmeg, big hard brown seeds about ¾ of an inch thick and high, has a great affinity for vegetables. Cloves add zest to stews and braised dishes. Many of these recipes tell you to add an onion, stuck with two or three cloves, during the long process. Paprika is another spice, and ranges from very hot to sweet in its pungency. One Hungarian cook I know has an entire range of paprikas for his cooking, obtained from the Paprikas-Weiss Store, 1504 Second Avenue, New York, N.Y., who send catalogues and ship by mail. The domestic paprika on the supermarket shelves has almost no flavor and merely adds color. Sometimes you want that color, for eye appeal, but for flavor, the imported Hungarian is truly essential when the recipe calls for paprika as an ingredient, not just a decoration.

Saffron is another spice, and one of the most interesting. It is probably the most expensive one in the world, costing over $300 a pound. It is the dried stigmas of a *Crocus sativus,* a plant grown mainly in Spain. Each tiny stigma must be picked by hand and laid carefully to dry. After drying, they are called threads. In the last few years, saffron threads have become almost impossible to buy; you can only find an expensive 6-inch jar with a teeny envelope of powdered saffron threads in it. After my first cookbook, a lady wrote me with a humorous but serious question. I had said "1 tablespoon of saffron" in a recipe. She had estimated the cost of 1 tablespoon of powdered saffron; it was over $12. I had, of course, meant the threads, which would have cost about 50 cents. But for certain dishes you must have it, even if it is only a tiny pinch of the powder (much more concentrated, of course, than the threads), for the distinctive color and heavenly flavor it imparts.

Chili powder is a blend of spices. The best one to buy is Gebhardt's. If you can't find it or get your favorite market to order it, then don't make things that call for chili powder as a seasoning. Or ask someone of Latin-American background to tell you about using the many varied fresh chilis. They are amazingly full of vitamins and minerals, too, which is a bonus.

Curry powder is also a blend of spices. In India, spices are hand-ground and used in different combinations, according to which meat, fish, or fowl will dominate the dish. We don't take that much trouble in our country. But if you like curries, it is well worth while to track down the very best imported curry powder. My choice is made by Venetchelli, and has a very crudely printed black and white paper wrapping around the can. If you can't find that, do try to get one imported from India. Domestic curry powders are, so far as I have tested, comparatively blah.

Now we come to the wonderful AROMATIC VEGETABLES AND ROOTS. This includes onions, to start with: red, yellow, white. The big red Spanish ones are sweet; in thin rings they add flavor and color to a salad. Sliced paper thin, alternated with equally thin orange slices, drizzled with good olive oil and sprinkled with coarse ground black pepper, they are just about my favorite salad. The yellows are generally mild, and what one wants mostly for cooking. The large whites are sharper and more pungent, and the little white onions for boiling can be a vegetable in themselves or add their savor to many other dishes.

Then we have garlic, usually sold in a bulb of cloves. I must always be careful that word is cloves, because I once went into print with "add one glove of garlic." (I've also never lived down a recipe for little pastry cups that read "This recipe will make 24 small smells.") Garlic is totally indispensable in the kitchen. And it must be, as must onion, used *fresh,* although I do use flash-frozen chopped raw onion in a pinch. But any form of *dried* onion or garlic is merely rancid to the taste. I repeat: any form. This includes the salts, the dried, the purées. The highly volatile oils in these vegetable roots go stale very rapidly. And few things are worse than rancid, stale onion or garlic flavor.

The leek is a very subtle and delicate member of the onion group. Often ignored by—or perhaps baffling to—Americans, it is a staple in every French kitchen and so beloved in Wales that it is their national symbol. In shape and color, it is similar to our green onions (scallions) but much, much fatter and bigger. Leeks can be braised as a vegetable, used to flavor almost any stew or soup, and were the inspiration and soul of Vichyssoise when Louis Diat, head chef at the Ritz in New York, remembered his mother's hearty French country potato-and-leek soup and refined it into the suave, chilled delicacy we know today. Last fall I made the original, from M. Diat's Maman's recipe, about a gallon of it, thinking to freeze most of it against the winter. The young man who zips in and out of here, and will sometimes eat with us if I'm fast with a lasso, just couldn't get enough of it. It was all gone in less than a week! I have also been known to whir it in a blender, heat it and add a can of minced clams at the very last. They made the best clam chowder my Philadelphian husband claimed *he'd* ever eaten. So I have great love for the leek.

Eschallots, or shallots, are a kind of cross, one might say, between the onion and garlic. They have their own distinctive flavor, but look like brown garlic cloves, their outer skin ranging from tan to brown to almost purple. They should always be peeled, minced and sautéed gently in a little butter before adding to a dish, and no French cook will be without them. If you can't find them, or afford them at 60 cents a little basket (they *do* keep well), you can always substitute the white parts of green onions. The dish won't taste quite the same, but the little green onion is better than nothing when you can't afford shallots.

Chives are another delicate member of the onion family, and are usually used as a garnish that adds flavor as well. They're sold in little pots in the markets, and look like a handful of long grass sticking up. Nothing makes me more convinced of an inferior restaurant than to be asked if I want sour-cream-and-chives on a baked potato and find minced stems of green onions instead of chives. They are not the same and don't taste the same. If you can't get them fresh or grow them, the flash-freeze dried are next best. Skip the dried ones in bottles.

Fresh ginger also belongs in the aromatic-root classification, and it becomes more widely available all the time. These roots are about an inch thick, have tan skin, are gnarled and usually branch into three or four "fingers." Most recipes of Oriental background call for "minced fresh ginger," usually a slice off the root, about the size of a quarter. In a little jar or plastic wrap, it keeps indefinitely in the freezer and can be sliced or grated off easily as needed. (Or pack slices into a small jar, pour in sherry or gin to cover, top with a lid or foil, and keep on a shelf in the refrigerator.) There is just no substitute for its fresh flavor. Dried ginger is often substituted, but when the fresh is so easy to get nowadays and so easy to keep on hand, why not use the real thing? Fresh ginger root can be found in neighborhood grocery stores where there is a large Chinese or Puerto Rican population, and is now being stocked by chain supermarkets.

Even the six supermarkets within a two-mile range of the tiny town in Utah where I live all have it.

Mustard is the final *spice,* the dried seeds of a plant, that you use almost constantly. And while there are many ranges of heat in it, Colman's, in the yellow box, is the general all-purpose one to buy in dried form. You can make *hot* mustard from it, too, by mixing into a paste with stale beer and letting it sit. The longer it sits, the hotter it gets; eaten carefully in tiny dabs on Chinese food, it is one of the real sinus-clearers I've yet discovered. "Wet" mustard, that ubiquitous paste spread on hot dogs, can also range from bland to hot, but most good cooks prefer the one made with white wine from Dijon, for all-round cooking.

There are two other things we should discuss in this chapter. One is monosodium glutamate, sold under various trade names such as MSG, Accent, Mei Yen, Ajinomoto (in Japanese stores), and Taste Powder (in Chinese stores). It was first discovered in Japan hundreds of years ago, and used *discreetly* to enhance the flavors of meat, fish, fowl and vegetables. It is much overused today, I think. Almost every packaged and prepared product lists it among the ingredients, but if you have decent vegetables and meat, you don't really need it in everything. At the most, you need a little pinch, about ⅛ teaspoon, if you use it. Do try to find a store that sells Oriental foods exclusively. I paid less than a dollar for a whole pound of Ajinomoto when last I bought it several years ago. The commercially named brands cost *at least* three to four times as much. Monosodium glutamate can also cause the so-called Chinese restaurant syndrome when used too freely. This rather exotic-sounding and harmless malady is a feeling of tightness in the skin of the head and in the jaw. It passes off after a few hours.

The other powder is meat tenderizer. This is an extract of the papaya plant, and comes to us from the South Seas, where the natives long ago learned that meat and fowl wrapped in papaya leaves and baked in their pits became very tender. This, again, is violently overused, and the seasoned ones are an abomination to a good cook. When it was first introduced in this country, I had a friend working in an advertising agency. Her boss, not believing the manufacturer's claims for the product, procured a piece of cheap steak, sprinkled it liberally with the tenderizer, and went out to a long lunch with some clients. When he returned, about four in the afternoon, the steak was just a mass of pulp all over his desk. The enzymes in the product had done their work, too well. I use a tenderizer, of course, but seldom and sparingly. I don't want the insides of my tummy tenderized to a pulp. Neither should you. If you use about one-quarter to one-half the amount the package tells you, it can be valuable. Just remember that the heat of cooking speeds up the enzyme action. *They* don't tell you that! And most of the meat that you can buy commercially today has already been treated with it, anyway. A bookkeeping friend who had several meat-processing firms as clients told me that, in sheer horror. (She had to pay the bills for it for her clients.)

There are numerous other herbs and spices, and as you cook, you will discover many, many more than the ones I have talked about here. I merely want to get you introduced to the basics, their distinctions and their major uses. Then you can go exploring on your own. It adds great fun to your cooking.

10 The Emergency Shelf

This is not a stockpiling of food against plague, famine, or depression but a discussion of foods that can be used to make cocktail or late-night snacks, to make a main dish for unexpected guests, and to prepare brunches for overnight guests as well. A list of emergency foods and recipes.

I have purposely kept the list below as short as possible. It is not supposed to be a list of kitchen basics, which you have sense enough to supply for yourself. But for the time when you decide that *you* are the emergency, and need a steaming mug of thick, hot soup to take to bed and relax with, I've listed the ones I keep: potato soup and split pea soup. I assume that you keep such things as bread, eggs, milk, olive oil, butter, seasonings, various kinds of crackers, etc., on hand. So the list that follows is what I keep, over and beyond basics. From it you can make a paella to serve as a dinner, or a Hangtown Fry for a brunch, and all the other things I've given you the recipes for, without running to the store.

FROM THE FREEZER

cube steaks
ground chuck
creamed spinach
peas
chicken parts
raw shrimp
crab meat

fish fillets
knockwurst or large barbecue
    franks
potato soup
orange juice
French rolls
French or Italian bread

FROM THE SHELVES

canned oysters
minced clams
clams with shells
Gebhardt's Chili
Gebhardt's Tamales
onion soup
anchovy fillets
chopped spinach
whole green chilis
minced green chilis
deviled ham
small whole cooked potatoes
olives, both black and green
tuna
pimentos, whole and sliced

brick-oven baked beans
tomatoes, whole, sliced, in sauce
    and purée
tomato juice
split-pea soup
chicken broth, cubes or granules
beef broth, cubes or granules
liver spread or pâté
spaghetti sauce seasoning in a
    packet
corned beef
corned-beef hash
roast-beef hash
mushrooms, whole and in bits-and-
    pieces

sliced almonds
Welsh rabbit in jars or cans
red caviar
sardines

hot-roll mix
enriched spaghetti, #2 or vermicelli
enriched noodles, medium size
rice, both instant and long-grain

CHEESES

grated Parmesan cheese in a *jar*
Romano, to grate fresh and rewrap
   tightly
cream cheese
sharp cheddar

Monterey jack
Swiss (domestic or imported)
Roquefort or Danish Blue
Rouge et Noir Breakfast Cheese

For many years, in a happy house in South Laguna, to which was eventually added a little guest cottage, I really learned about the value of brunch.
It is a horrid word, but it has sneaked into our language and there is no
other that describes the meal I mean. It is the one you feed guests who
stagger out in mid-morning, bleary-eyed and quivering, so you have lots
of coffee, hot and strong enough to raise up and flag a train, and juices
with a shot of vodka in them to bring the alcoholic content of the blood
back to normal after a night of dancing at what we called the Dirty Bar in
Dana Point. That was not its real name, of course, but it had great jazz, a
roof that went up and down when the surfers began doing their stomp, a
couple of very pretty and available girls, and a *gentleman* who ran it with
great aplomb. My weekend guests who I thought would appreciate it, both
the music and the fantastic dancing, always came out still slightly shaking
in the morning. And while they drank their coffee and juices, I made brunch
—filling, nourishing and satisfying, calming to the nerves and making one
believe one will live again. Brunch is also a very easy and relaxed way of
entertaining, for single girls or young couples without much money and
with lots of friends who entertain them. So included in this chapter are all
the recipes that were favorites over those years, plus others since discovered to be of therapeutic aid.

   As for the late-night snack, it has, I am sure, saved many a life. During
my years in Los Angeles, many friends who lived up in the canyons and
gave parties always provided late-night food. One friend discovered, after
many years of making his own onion soup ahead of time, that the kind that

comes in the familiar half-red and half-white can, with about one table-spoon of bourbon added for each two servings, is considered "his best." And I will give you a recipe for his Welsh Rabbit, although many good ones come in bottles and cans. (It *is* a rabbit, not a rarebit. In Wales, when the husband went out to get a rabbit for dinner, the thoughtful wife always had the ingredients in store to make a cheese one should he come home empty-handed.) At any rate in this chapter you will find recipes you can start ahead and finish when necessary.

I approach the subject of the omelet with great trepidation. Whole *books* have been written on the subject. However, I do make them, they come out fine, and they're a perfect brunch or late-night food.

There are two kinds of omelet—the French and the puffy. We'll deal with the French one first. Years ago, Dione Lucas had a luncheon restaurant in New York, where she made each omelet to order, in about three minutes. I would get a table as close to her as possible, and *watch*. (It is the best possible way to learn how to cook.) There are three essential tricks. One is the pan, one is the heat, and one the way to turn the omelet out of the pan.

So here we go: The pan should be about 8 to 9 inches across, of heavy iron, steel, or enamel over metal. It should have sloping sides and a good long handle. Mine is a La Creuset, and it is never washed, merely wiped out with paper towels after each use. There is now on the market a kind of nonstick lined variety of pots and pans; you must use only wooden utensils with them, or specially-marked-for-them ones. I have never found any of them satisfactory. There is also a spray product that is supposed to stop sticking. It won't work for me, either, although I assume it does for many other people. But there is no such thing as the perfect omelet pan for *everybody.* Altitude, climate, your stove, your kind of heat, the age of your eggs and your *hands* have much to do with it, just as they do with good bread, or pie crust, or any other so-called temperamental foods.

I've heard people discuss omelets by the hour. Because I was told by every reliable cookbook I know, and Dione Lucas, I only use this one La Creuset pan for them. But if I were hungry, and had only a chop to pan-broil, I would not hesitate to use that pan for it. And I am sure it would turn out a perfect omelet, next time. For *me,* it is a *reliable* pan.

Never try to make an omelet with more than three eggs. That will serve two people . . . or you can make a two-egg one, to be divided and the next made in about three minutes.

As for fillings, the list is endless. My favorite at Dione Lucas's restaurant used to be red caviar and sour cream. Or you can use ½ to ¾ cup of any of the following, to start with:

creamed chopped spinach
sautéed mushrooms
cooked asparagus tips
cooked crab, shrimp or lobster
diced ham
cooked, crumbled bacon
grated sharp cheddar cheese

grated Monterey jack cheese with
    sautéed onion, green pepper, and
    Tabasco
seasoned cooked tomatoes with
    green chilis, chopped, from a can
and so on . . .

THE BASIC OMELET

Serves 2

3 eggs
Pinch of salt

Generous tablespoon of butter
Filling, if desired

1. Beat the eggs very lightly with the salt, just enough to mix yolks and whites.

2. Heat your pan over a medium brisk flame and add the butter. When it turns golden and begins to give off what the French call a "nutty" smell, pour in eggs.

3. Let it cook for a moment or two, until it is set on the sides. With a spatula, lift up the set sides and tilt the pan to let the uncooked top run underneath.

4. Let cook a moment or two more, until the sides are set again and the center soft but lightly cooked. Spread on the filling, not quite to the edges.

5. Turn the pan so that the handle is on your left. Make a crease across the omelet, at right angles to the handle, with your spatula.

6. Put your left hand underneath the handle, palm up, and tilt the pan upward. With your right hand, slide the spatula under the portion near the handle and fold it over, lifting to help it fold. The folded omelet can

then be slid right out onto a warm plate and should be served at once.

note: For more than two people, you have to make more than one omelet. Increasing the recipe doesn't work.

THE PUFFY OMELET

Serves 2 to 3

5-6 *eggs*
¼ *teaspoon cream of tartar*
   Salt

5-6 *tablespoons cream*
1 *generous tablespoon butter*

1. Preheat oven to 450°.
2. Separate the eggs, the whites into one large bowl, the yolks into a smaller one. Beat the whites until stiff, adding the cream of tartar.
3. Beat the yolks, adding salt, until thick, then beat in the cream. (I always beat the whites first, because a speck of yolk in whites prevents them from rising as they should.)
4. As directed for soufflé, *fold* the yolk mixture into the whites with a spatula. Then slide this mixture into your hot omelet pan when the butter is nutty and golden, and cook over very low heat for ten minutes, until the bottom is golden but the top still moist-looking.
5. Quickly slide the omelet pan into the hot oven and bake for fifteen to twenty minutes, until top is puffed and browned lightly. Either fold it over like a regular omelet or cut in wedges to serve.

SWISS FONDUE

Serves 4

½ *pound grated or shredded* real
   Swiss cheese
1 *tablespoon flour*
1 *clove garlic*
1 *cup dry, white wine*
   Salt

Pepper
Nutmeg
3 *tablespoons kirsch*
   Sour-dough French bread, in
   1½-inch cubes, each with some
   crust

1. Add cheese to flour and mix together thoroughly.

2. Rub the inside of the pot or chafing dish thoroughly with a cut clove of garlic, pour in the wine and heat through.

3. When wine is almost boiling, add cheese and stir constantly with a fork until cheese is melted. Add salt, pepper, and a dash of nutmeg.

4. Bring to table, adjust heat to low, add kirsch and stir in, keeping the fondue just barely simmering gently.

note: You will need a chafing dish with controllable flame or a fondue pot. Start the fondue in the kitchen and finish it at the table.

to serve: Each guest spears a piece of bread through the crust and dips into the fondue, stirring to keep the fondue simmering. Everybody takes turns. This is the traditional fondue.

serve with: The same dry white wine you used in the fondue, and melon for dessert with coffee.

CHILES RELLENOS FOR BRUNCH

Serves 4

2 *four-ounce cans roasted whole green chilis*
4 *ounces Monterey jack cheese, in one piece*
Flour

8 *eggs*
4 *tablespoons butter*
Salt
Pepper

1. Open the cans of chilis and carefully separate them. Slit each lengthwise and, under cold running water, remove seeds.

2. Cut the cheese into domino-sized pieces, one for each chili, and wrap in the chili. Roll each in flour, and set aside, to dry slightly.

3. Beat the eggs lightly. Melt the butter in a skillet large enough to hold the chilis and sauté them gently, turning with two wooden spoons, until lightly browned all over.

4. Pour in the beaten eggs, over and around the chilis, season with salt and pepper. As the eggs set, carefully lift around the edges, tipping the pan, to let uncooked eggs run under. When eggs look almost done, care-

fully turn each chili with a spatula and cook about 1 minute more. Serve at once on warmed plates.

serve with: Pre-brunch drinks with fresh pineapple wedges, refried beans, and little heat-and-serve sausages or sautéed lamb kidneys, and warmed tortillas. Lots of strong black coffee goes with this, and perhaps a little brandy in the coffee for those who want it.

CHILI AND TAMALES

Serves 2

1 can Gebhardt's Chili   ¼ cup chopped onion
1 can Gebhardt's Tamales

    1. Heat chili and tamales separately.
    2. With tongs, take tamales from pan and divide between two plates, removing paper covering.
    3. Spoon hot chili over and sprinkle with freshly chopped onion.

serve with: Small glasses of tequila and of Sangrita, with corn chips and a packaged avocado dip to start, heated tortillas with the chili and tamales, and a big platter of fresh fruit bites with coffee for dessert.

CLAMS CASINO

Serves 4

24 clams on half shell   ¼ cup chopped parsley
    Rock salt   ½ cup fine dry bread crumbs
½ cup butter   Lemon juice
⅓ cup chopped shallots, green   Tabasco
    onions or chives

    1. Heat oven to 450°.
    2. Arrange 6 clams each in 4 aluminum pie shells on beds of rock salt.
    3. Blend together the butter, shallots, and parsley with the bread crumbs. Divide evenly over clams and add a squeeze of lemon to each clam.

4. Bake until crumbs are toasted and clams heated through. Give each clam a dash of Tabasco and serve at once.

serve with: Brunch drinks and fresh fruit bites to start, crusty French sourdough bread, sweet butter. Coffee for those who want it.

The wine should be a light, dry, fruity white, such as a dry California Sauterne.

EASY EGGS BENEDICT

Serves 2

1 *six-ounce bottle or small can*	2 *English muffins*
hollandaise sauce	4 *slices boiled ham*
2 *tablespoons butter*	4 *eggs*
½ *teaspoon lemon juice*	

1. Preheat oven to 350°.

2. Put hollandaise into double boiler, or in small pot set into a larger one with about 1 inch water in bottom. Add 1 tablespoon butter and ½ teaspoon lemon juice, stirring to mix well. Let heat gently.

3. Split muffins, hollow out centers to form cups, and toast lightly under broiler flame. Butter well.

4. Place a slice of boiled ham on each muffin half and push down to keep cup form. Arrange on ovenproof serving dish.

5. Break an egg into each muffin-ham cup and bake until eggs are set. Pour warm hollandaise equally over each egg and serve at once.

serve with: A platter of mixed fresh fruit with drinks to start, salad with cucumbers and Tart French Dressing (page 76), frozen cheesecake with coffee.

The wine should be a light, dry white.

BAKED EGGS FIRENZE

Serves 4

Butter	*Pepper*
2 boxes frozen creamed spinach, cooked	*¼ cup plus 2 tablespoons grated Parmesan cheese*
8 eggs	*Tabasco*
Salt	*4 large tomatoes*
	Basil

1. Preheat oven to 350°.
2. Butter a large oven-to-table baking dish. Spread cooked spinach evenly in dish and with a wooden spoon make eight holes in the spinach.
3. Drop a raw egg into each hole, sprinkle with salt, pepper, and Parmesan. Place a drop of Tabasco on each egg yolk.
4. Oil another baking dish. Cut the tomatoes in half, set in the dish, and sprinkle with salt, pepper, and a pinch of dried, crushed basil leaves. Dot with butter.
5. Place eggs in oven and tomatoes under the broiler. Bake about eight minutes, or until the eggs are set and tomatoes broiled.

serve with: Screwdrivers, or Bloody Marys, to begin with; crusty French bread with the food; and an assortment of cheese and fruit to end.
The wine, if you serve one, should be a chilled dry white.

ONION SOUP

Serves 2

1 can Onion Soup, in the good old familiar red and white can	*4 thick slices toasted French bread*
2 tablespoons brandy or bourbon	*½ cup shredded Parmesan cheese*

1. Heat the soup, adding a little less water than the can directions say, and adding brandy or (preferably) bourbon.
2. Put toasted French bread in the bottom of deep soup bowls and ladle soup over.
3. Sprinkle cheese on top of toasted bread as it rises to the top and

serve. Nothing more is needed (unless a second helping) as a late-night, sobering, soporific snack.

There was once, in early California, a settlement called Hangtown. The vigilantes and posses took their prisoners there to be hanged. And it was part of the custom of the times to give the condemned man anything he wanted for his last dinner.

One smart cookie demanded Eastern oysters, cooked with scrambled eggs and bacon. Eggs were scarce and very expensive. So was bacon. And *Eastern* oysters in an edible condition were impossible to get across the country. They finally had to let him go free, and thus the name of the dish came about—Hangtown Fry. I first ate it in San Francisco, at Tadish's Grill. It still tastes wonderful to me: full of happy memories after all these years. It makes a marvelous brunch for lovers, or for anybody else in need of real nourishment.

THE CLASSIC HANGTOWN FRY

Serves 2

An 8-ounce can oysters
Flour
1 beaten egg
½ cup fine dry bread crumbs
½ stick butter

4 slices bacon, halved and cooked
5 large eggs
Salt
Pepper
Tabasco

1. Dip oysters individually in flour, then in beaten eggs, then in bread crumbs.
2. Melt butter in a skillet and sauté oysters one minute on each side.
3. Arrange cooked bacon slices in skillet with oysters.
4. Beat the eggs with salt, pepper, and a dash of Tabasco. Pour in the seasoned beaten egg mixture and cook over low flame until eggs are set, gently lifting the sides of this "omelet" to let uncooked eggs run underneath. Slide it under a broiler flame to brown top lightly and serve at once.

A SALAD FROM THE RIVIERA

Serves 4

1 *head romaine or Boston lettuce*
4 *medium tomatoes, skinned and quartered*
1 *cup cooked whole green beans, fresh or canned*
1 *8½-ounce can small whole potatoes, drained and sliced*
2 *hard-boiled eggs, quartered*
1 *red or brown mild onion, sliced paper thin*

1 *green pepper, in matchstick slices*
8 *anchovy fillets, drained and snipped in small pieces*
12 *pitted black olives*
1 *7½-ounce can chunk tuna, drained and broken into pieces*
 Classic French Dressing (page 76)

1. Line a large platter with the lettuce, then arrange rows of the above ingredients to make a colorful, inviting picture.
2. Pour dressing over the salad. Chill for at least half an hour.
3. Bring to the table and toss thoroughly before serving.

serve with: Jellied consommé with lemon wedges to start, French bread and sweet butter, and frozen cheesecake or a sherbet for dessert.
The wine should be a dry white, a rosé, or a very light red.

SCRAMBLED EGGS (WITH ADDITIONS)

Serves 4

8 *to 10 eggs*
1 *tablespoon cream for each egg*
½ *teaspoon baking powder*
2 *tablespoons butter*

1 *flat can anchovy fillets, drained (optional)*
1 *3-ounce package cream cheese, cubed (optional)*

1. Beat eggs lightly with a fork and add cream and baking powder.
2. Melt butter in the top of a double boiler over (but not in) simmering water. Add either the anchovy fillets, snipped in pieces, OR the cream cheese cut in cubes, to the lightly beaten eggs. NOTE: If dealing with more than 4 eggs, break each one into a cup first; nothing in the world is worse

than adding the twelfth egg to what will be scrambled eggs for a late-night snack, and finding it black. I *know*.

3. Pour egg and seasonings mixture into the top of the double boiler, and as they start to cook, stir with a wooden spoon, carefully scraping bottom and sides in large sections. When eggs are finished—set but still soft and gentle—serve on warmed plates.

serve with: If it is to be brunch, you will find that little precooked sausages are good, and cook while you hover over the eggs, and you'll want hot rolls of some kind. If it is late-at-night snack time, mere toast will satisfy most people.

The wine should be a light dry white for brunch. Coffee for late-nighters.

SPANISH DEVILED OMELET

Serves 4

1 *medium onion, diced fine*
1 *medium green pepper, diced fine*
1 *tablespoon olive oil*
   A 4½-ounce can deviled ham
1 *medium tomato, skinned and diced*
2 *tablespoons butter*

4 *dashes Tabasco*
8 *eggs, beaten lightly*
½ *teaspoon salt*
¼ *teaspoon pepper*
1 *tomato, skinned and quartered*

1. Sauté diced onion and pepper in oil until tender. Add deviled ham and diced tomato, and keep warm over low heat.

2. Melt butter in a large heavy skillet, add Tabasco to beaten eggs, add salt and pepper and pour into skillet over medium heat. As omelet begins to set, carefully lift edges with a spatula and let uncooked portion run under.

3. When omelet is set but top is still soft, pour deviled ham mixture over and spread evenly with a spatula. Cook one minute more.

4. Cut omelet into wedges and garnish each with a tomato quarter. Serve at once, on warm plates.

serve with: A platter of antipasto with beginning drinks, a salad of avocado and orange slices drizzled with olive oil and coarse black pepper, and lime sherbet with a little crème de menthe poured over for dessert.

The wine should be a light red claret.

SPEDINI, MY WAY

Serves 4

1 *long loaf French or Italian bread*
1 *stick butter*
2-3 *tablespoons Dijon mustard*
1 *tablespoon poppy or sesame*
   seeds

½ *pound sliced* real *Swiss cheese*
1 *small flat can anchovies or 4*
   slices bacon, cut in half

1. Preheat oven to 350°.

2. Trim off most of the crust from the top and sides of the bread, and slash almost to the bottom at 1-inch intervals.

3. Cream the butter with the mustard and poppy or sesame seeds and spread generously down between the slashes of bread.

4. Insert the slices of cheese and a strip of anchovy between the slashes. If bacon is used, arrange on top of the loaf. Bake until cheese is melted and loaf hot.

serve with: Salty Dogs (vodka and grapefruit juice) to start, a tossed green salad with Classic French Dressing (page 76), and a bowl of mixed fresh fruits with a sour-cream dressing for dessert with coffee.

SPINACH-CHEESE SOUFFLÉ

Serves 4

2 *tablespoons butter*
2 *tablespoons flour*
1 *cup hot milk*
   Salt
4 *egg yolks, beaten*

1 *7½-ounce can chopped*
   spinach, well-drained
½ *cup grated cheese, preferably*
   sharp Cheddar
6 *egg whites, beaten stiff*

1. Preheat oven to 350°.

2. In a saucepan, over medium heat, melt the butter, stir in the flour, and cook for a few moments. Then add the milk all at once and stir madly to incorporate, then cook gently until sauce is thick and smooth.

3. Add a light dash of salt. Pour a little of the sauce into the beaten egg yolks to warm them, then add the yolks a little at a time to the sauce, off the fire, stirring constantly. Add spinach and cheese and return to heat,

continuing to stir, until sauce is smooth again. Let mixture cool a bit, about ten minutes.

4. Carefully *fold* this mixture into the beaten egg whites. *Do not stir.* Pour this mixture gently into a straight-sided, ungreased soufflé dish or casserole. Run the edge of a small spatula or knife around the edge of the dish, about 1½ inches in from the rim, to make a "high hat" when finished.

5. Bake soufflé for forty to fifty minutes, until top is firm to the touch of your finger. Rush at once to table, and serve with a warmed spoon.

serve with: Pre-brunch drinks and fruit bites, hot butterflake rolls, and lots of strong black coffee.

LATE-NIGHT STEAK SANDWICHES

Serves 4

1 beef or chicken bouillon cube	1 tablespoon cooking oil
1 cup hot water	2 cube steaks, preferably unfrozen
½ cup chili sauce	Salt
½ teaspoon Worcestershire sauce	Pepper
2 drops Tabasco	4 crusty French or onion rolls, split
1 medium onion, chopped	

1. Combine bouillon cube, water, chili sauce, Worcestershire, and Tabasco in a small pan. Simmer gently to blend well.

2. Sauté onion gently in oil until golden. Remove and add to sauce. You can cool sauce at this point, and reheat ½ hour before serving.

3. One-half hour before serving, cut steaks in half, season them, and sear in a heated black iron skillet that is lightly salted. Pour sauce over, cover, and simmer gently for twenty to thirty minutes.

4. Dip cut sides of rolls in sauce, place a piece of steak on each, and cover with top half of roll.

serve with: Lots of coffee, or small glasses of dry red wine as a nightcap drink.

WELSH RABBIT

Serves 4

 2 *tablespoons butter*
¾ *teaspoon salt*
½ *teaspoon dry mustard*
¾ *pound sharp Cheddar, grated*

¾ *cup beer or ale*
1 *egg, well beaten*
Toasted, buttered English muffin
halves

1. Melt butter over medium heat in a saucepan. Add seasonings and cheese.

2. Cook over gentle heat until cheese is melted, stirring constantly.

3. Stir in beer or ale and mix well. Just before serving, stir in egg and mix again.

4. Pour over toasted, buttered English muffin halves.

11 Wines—What You Need to Know About Them to Begin With

General types of wines. The right glasses. Wine as a
hobby. The pitfalls of pretension and wine snobbery.
The uses of liqueurs.

Wine is good for you. It helps the digestion. It is a complex, constantly changing substance, but understanding how to drink wines is essentially simple. They come in red, white, and rosé; sweet and dry; sparkling and still. Some—such as sherry, port, marsala, and Madeira—are fortified with brandy which is added during production. That's it.

Because we as a nation do not have a long history of wine use and grape cultivation, the mystery and ritual surrounding wine have intimidated many of us. Knowledge about wine has built up over thousands of years, and we come newly to it, with our Puritan ancestors lurking gloomily in the background. All this talk about vintage years and château bottlings, varietals and generics, has too long prevented many of us from enjoying the pleasure and satisfaction of a glass of wine with our dinner. I hope, in this chapter, to dispel some of the illusions and to interest you in the exploration of a subject that will enhance your culinary pleasure and your palate.

Americans usually stick to the basic rule that you serve dry wines with the main courses, no wine at all with the salad course if the salad has vinegar in its dressing, and sweeter wines with dessert.

It is a general rule that whites are served with fish and light meats, reds with red meat. And a rosé will go with almost anything. (But like all rules, there are exceptions . . . with a Coq au Vin, you serve the same red you cooked him in.) I once heard two brothers, who were considered among the greatest vintners in France, say at a wine forum, "He likes red, I like white" . . . so that's what they had with their lunch. Their advice was, "If you like it, drink it!" at informal meals.

The "fortified wines" are generally drunk as apéritifs, or with desserts, and they are widely used in cooking. I myself prefer, if possible, to add them toward the end of the cooking period. And if you use brandy for flaming a dish, it should first be gently heated, to release the alcohol fumes.

The second rule of thumb is that whites and rosés are served chilled, and reds at room temperature after they have been opened and had a chance to "breathe" and release their bouquet. That's the whole purpose of the "breathing" process. But in this country we have some very reasonably priced reds—what the French call "le vin ordinaire," such as Paisano and Spañada—that I prefer chilled. I'd rather drink them than no wine at all with my meal.

In this country, dessert wines are almost never served except at formal dinners. Port has an affinity for a big bowl of walnuts, and a charming Englishwoman once explained to me why the ladies leave the table and the gentlemen to their port. The ladies withdraw to get a chance at the bathroom. Then when the gentlemen join them, demitasse coffee and brandy or liqueurs are served.

It is increasingly being acknowledged that there are, in addition to the wines of Europe, *good* American wines. Certain vintners are truly reliable, and often their products are better than cheap imports. My theory and feeling is that if you want to investigate wines, you should start with a small selection and find out what you like. In many sections of the country where the wine industry flourishes, wine-tasting shops are being set up. Wine can be·a very pleasant hobby, if approached sensibly according to your budget.

Let's start with a basic American collection, and by all means a notebook in which you write down what you buy and what you think of it. Here's a basic list:

1 bottle dry cocktail sherry	1 bottle California Zinfandel (dry white)
½ gallon California dry red	
½ gallon California dry white	1 bottle California Pinot Noir (a dry red tending more toward a burgundy)
1 bottle Riesling	
1 bottle rosé	
1 bottle Chianti	
1 bottle California Cabernet (light red, similar to a claret)	

Dry whites will bear such names as Pinot Blanc, Pinot Chardonnay, Sauvignon Blanc, Sémillon, and Traminer. And the best come from such vintners as Almadén, Beaulieu, Inglenook, Krug, Martinini, Masson, and in New York, Widmer.

Reds are Cabernet, Zinfandel, and Pinot Noir. The Cabernets and Zinfandels are usually lighter and more equal to a claret than the Pinot Noirs, which range from (in comparing them with imports) Bordeaux to Burgundy.

The same vintners that I listed above make both reds and whites.

The rosés are in still another category, but Almadén has won many international prizes for its product, just as Wente has for its Grey Riesling.

Champagne reigns as the most festive of wines, and you can buy it in sizes from a little split to a Nebuchadnezzar, holding twenty quarts. It is a restorative to the soul and a friend in need. I am reliably told, but have never known this luxury, that a diet of champagne and caviar will keep you from being seasick. I do know that a little split from the nearest liquor store has helped me to cope with some of my direst emergencies. And a wonderful dowager I once knew would feed me Great Western's Champagne Brut when she thought I needed it. From long experience, I know that on nights when it grows late and lonely, and that thick black cloud of depression hovers over you, there is nothing like a quick shower, the prettiest nightgown, and a split of champagne to take to bed. It is the most elegant nightcap in the world, and makes me feel like an elegant lady.

What you drink wine *from* is important to its true enjoyment. The classic tulip shape is always right. There are valid reasons. The stem and the rounded bowl enable you to swirl the wine around to release its bouquet; the slight curve in at the top enables you to enjoy that bouquet. Tulip-shaped wine glasses can be found in a price range from 39 cents on up to $50 a glass. So if you are going to drink wine, there's no reason why you shouldn't drink it from a glass that was designed to give you the best of it. One thing everybody agrees upon, however, is that a wine glass should *never* be of colored or cut glass. It must be clear, so that the color of the wine is not obscured.

Should you want to have truly beautiful wine glasses at a reasonable price, I suggest that you write Esquin Imports, 119 Sacramento Street, San Francisco, California 94111, for their catalogue. Their burgundy glasses are the most exquisite I have ever seen—big round globes like soap bubbles, on a stem that is just right for balancing in the hand. (Nothing is worse than too high a stem.) I've had mine for over twelve years, so for all their seeming fragility, they are sturdy. And I use mine for all wines, because they are so lovely. Half a dozen will cost you around $11, or at least that is what they cost the last time I sent some for a wedding present.

Another thing that can give you and your friends great pleasure, and make even simple desserts seem festive, is a collection of liqueurs. Admittedly, they are expensive, but you can buy small bottles. To start with, I'd suggest the following:

crème de menthe
Chartreuse (the green kind, not the
yellow)
kirsch
Kahlúa
Cointreau

Benedictine
B and B (a mixture of Benedictine
and brandy)
brandy
crème de cacao

You can go on from there; the list is endless and fun to explore. You will need small glasses for liqueurs, and you pour them only about half full. I have some teardrop-shaped ones from Steuben, heavy at the bottom so they won't tip, and when half full (I just measured) they contain one tablespoon. That's quite enough to sip and savor with after-dinner coffee.

If you get interested in wines as a hobby, there are many books on the subject that will guide and help you. Alexis Lichine has written the definitive book on the wines of France.* There are many other comprehensive and good books on American wines as well. Among your best friends could be a wine shop run by a man who knows and loves his wares and who's willing to talk about them by the hour, to help educate you.

I have merely skimmed the surface here, to try to remove some of the mystique and cultism from the subject and to get you started in investigating wines for yourself without wondering whether you are right or wrong. *Salut!* Even the Scriptures say, "Use a little wine for thy stomach's sake."

* *The Wines of France* (New York: Alfred A. Knopf).

Finale: A Personal Philosophy

In all honesty, I must admit that I didn't set out to be a cook, because there were at least three professions I would have chosen instead. I was going to be a dress designer, a jazz pianist, or a writer. But when I grew up, during the depression of the thirties, one was lucky to get through high school. Education for a designer was out of the question. So my first job was in a record shop where I could be around music, and in my spare time I started writing, having taken tests and discovered that I was rhythmically deficient and could not play a three in one hand against a four in the other.

I can't remember a time when I couldn't sew or cook. My first memory of cooking is when my grandmother took care of me for the afternoon. I made flour-and-water paste and colored it with mustard and turmeric (used in Utah for pickles, as are all sorts of other exotic spices never used in *cooking*). My little "cookies" came out a beautiful saffron color, and I was disappointed when the chickens wouldn't eat them. Discovering this, Mother said, "Let her cook along with you, then, if she's so interested." So I stood on a wooden box and did what Grandmother did. It turned out to be lemon-meringue pie. We also made doll clothes together, so I learned to sew by hand and eventually graduated to the treadle Singer sewing machine. These were considered the normal accomplishments for our pioneer society. You could cook, you could sew, or you were retarded or lazy. Retarded brought no shame, but lazy, well! The parents were pitied for such a child. Helping Grandmother with the desserts—for no meal in those times was complete without cake or pie—I learned the hardest things first. Cooking was just a job I'd grown into, loved, and could take off my mother's hands. As the only child, it also enabled me to bask in

Daddy's approval, which any girl in a male-oriented society wants. If "The Babe" made it, it was undoubtedly the best ever eaten.

It has been over two years now since I made a lemon-meringue pie, or a black devil's-food cake with inch-thick frosting. I do know that now when I make our old-fashioned oatmeal cookies, full of raisins and nuts (I double the amount the recipe calls for) and spices, to feed a young man who needs the nourishment, they disappear with great rapidity. They are real, not synthetic. They are wolfed down, as is the bread we make, which bears no resemblance whatsoever to the soggy cotton that comes in waxed-paper packages. If bread is soft, I won't buy it. We make honest bread and honest food. I think that this is the secret of all good food: It must be made with real ingredients, not chemical substitutes, and it must be treated with respect for the nourishing qualities of its ingredients.

As a child I ate, of course, because I was hungry. As I grew up, I learned about a wider world of food and tastes than I'd ever learned on our farm. It was a wonderful world. You don't have to like everything in it. I do not like eel, for example. I have eaten it many different ways, and I still don't like it, no matter what they do to it. Nor do I like squid. Both seem to me about as rewarding as chewing on a slice of rubber hose. I object to the texture, and to me there is no compensating taste. But there are plenty of other foods that delight me.

Living back in Utah now, I yearn for Maine lobster and cherrystone clams. But in my freezer I have, at the moment, both venison and wild duck, of which I dreamed when I lived in Manhattan. And I am surrounded by three acres of apple, crabapple, peach, and plum trees. Plus bushel baskets of roses.

A few years ago, my cousin Lois and I, in a nostalgic mood, made an old-fashioned Sunday dinner. We made everything, except the pickles and jams, that we remembered as being good when we were children. I remembered helping Grandma chase down the chickens that she would fry, and the sour-cream gravy that she, being Danish, knew how to make from turned cream (the French call it crème fraîche). We had a deep, mysterious cellar, with a milk room where the big, wide blue enamel pans sat, and if Grandma was in a good mood, I was allowed to help skim off the cream. I still remember the taste of that gravy, ladled over tiny red new potatoes. I know now, too, how to make crème fraîche from heavy cream: heat it to warm, not hot, add a little yogurt or buttermilk, and let it stand, covered, until it thickens (about ten hours).

My cousin remembered all the jams and jellies and pickles, the pies and cakes, the fresh corn and peas and asparagus, the baking-soda biscuits, the hot yeast rolls, and the homemade ice cream which we kids all took turns cranking. Strictly supervised by an impartial adult, we were allowed licks on the dasher when it was removed and the cool wooden freezer carefully wrapped in gunny sacks against the end of the long summer day.

Lois and I made a foray to the Farmers' Market in Los Angeles, and after about two days we laid the whole thing out for her teen-agers and their friends in Beverly Hills. I never saw so much food disappear so fast. These were not deprived children. Far from it. Most of them had grown up fed by servants and given generous allowances to buy anything they wanted. So, obviously, they eat hamburgers, pizza, hot dogs, and tacos. One boy at our Sunday dinner said to me, "I just never *knew* there was food like this!" He was eating hot yeast rolls at the moment and his eyes were questing the table spread with other home-cooked food—you could still smell it coming out of the kitchen. It seemed sad to me.

I was even sadder when I got around to looking for something to eat myself. It was all gone. I suspect that the big platter we had been replenishing with crisp red-brown fried chicken had been *licked.* I know there were no crumbs left in the pie dishes or on the cake plates. Quite simply, they were starved for the taste of honest food.

I have never met anyone, rich or poor, if in good health, who did not respond with gusto to good food. How do you know your food is good? You taste it. If you watch Julia Child on television (and you should), you will see her tasting all the time.

Good cooks also use their hands—to knead doughs, to toss salads, to place pastry in pans.

Food prejudices can be most illogical. My mother, who happily cooks liver and sweetbreads, tongue and heart, turns a weird shade of yellow-green when confronted with a delicate little lamb kidney. The "why" is built into her; it is personal. I, on the other hand, will eat brains but under silent protest. Everyone to whom you serve food has his own personal likes and dislikes. It is only kind to ask ahead of time, "Do you like such-

and-such?," or, "Are you allergic to any food?" You also don't ask "why" of a guest who refuses a dish. But don't concern yourself over the guest who accepts an invitation to dinner and then refuses everything because he will eat only chicken. And you've got roast beef with cheese-stuffed baked potatoes. He doesn't eat cheese and his potatoes must be boiled. He should not go out to dine unless he first informs the hostess of his prejudices.

Fortunately, nowadays the prejudiced are much rarer than they once were.

If you are thoughtful and if *you* think the food tastes good, then be pleased with your food and your guests will share that pleasure with you. Good food nourishes the stomach and the soul.

Please, don't get shook up and feel failure if your guests don't eat everything in sight. And whoever paraphrased Shakespeare was wrong when he wrote "Distrust the lean and hungry cook." If you hang over pots and kettles inhaling fumes, and you taste constantly, you just aren't that hungry when the food gets on the table. Two of the truly great French chefs whose food I have had the pleasure of eating were Louis Diat and Henri Charpentier—both slat-thin. I am far more inclined to distrust the obese cook, who looks as though he would eat anything.

I try to make my food savory, with honest ingredients, nourishing and wholesome. So far, I think I have been reasonably successful. I have hopes for us all that we will all love and live long, in the enjoyment of what we eat and in the happiness that comes from having a well-nourished body.

Index

72 73 74 75 10 9 8 7 6 5 4 3 2 1